Tatyana McFadden

with Tom Walker

Ya Sama!
Moments from My Life

InspiredEdge
Editions

Produced by Storiport.net
www.storiport.net

Published by InspiredEdge Editions
www.ieeditions.com

ISBN-13: 978-0692696026
ISBN-10: 0692696024

Life is not about what you don't have,
but what you do with what you are given.

-Tatyana McFadden

CHAPTER 1

The Grand Slam

*V*rring! *Vrring!* The alarm clock rattles off. It's 4:20 a.m. I hit the snooze button and grab my phone to check the weather. It's near freezing outside, but the November skies are clear.

"Great! I won't have to worry about icy or wet roads today," I think to myself as I pull the blankets up around me and enjoy a few more minutes in bed contemplating the day ahead.

It's race day–the 2014 New York City marathon–the last major marathon of the year. It has been an exciting year for me so far. I've been blessed with a string of wins. I started

On the starting line of the NYC Marathon.

the year by competing in my first winter games, the Sochi Winter Paralympics, in Russia, and winning a silver medal in the one-kilometer cross-country skiing race. A few weeks later I won marathons in Boston and London, setting a new marathon course record in London. And in October I won the Chicago marathon.

If I win the marathon today, I win the Grand Slam, which is when one person wins the four biggest marathons in the world—Boston, Chicago, London, and New York—all in the same year. I won the Grand Slam last year, so if I win today's race, I will have achieved it two years in a row! No one—with or without a disability—has ever done this before.

"No pressure here!" I tell myself as my thoughts run to all the things that can go wrong. I've trained hard, and I have the course mapped out in my head. I remind myself to stay focused and have fun!

I pull myself out of bed and dress. I'm too anxious to eat much before a race, so I have only a little oatmeal and peanut butter. I check my racing chair and make sure I have everything I need.

By 6:00 a.m., I'm on the bus that takes me and some of the other racers to the start of the marathon at the base of the Verrazano Bridge. It's still dark when we arrive, and an almost-full moon hangs over the city. The early morning air is chilly, and there is a light wind. All the racers are stretching, trying to warm up. I start my own routine, getting my muscles ready.

What is a marathon?

The marathon is a long-distance running event with an official distance of 42.195 kilometers (26 miles and 385 yards). It is usually run as a road race through cities across the world, from Beijing to New York to Paris. The event commemorates the fabled run of Pheidippides, a messenger who ran 26 miles to deliver news of a Greek army's victory against the Persians in the Battle of Marathon.

Why is the distance not an even 26 miles? It is said that the distance was set to 26 miles and 385 yards because of the British royal family. During preparations for the 1908 summer Olympics, the organizers agreed to include a marathon of about 40 kilometers or 25 miles. British officials, wanting to please the King of England, planned the race to start at Windsor Castle and finish right in front of where the royal family would be sitting in the Olympic Stadium—a distance of precisely 26 miles and 385 yards.

I greet a few fellow racers and wish everyone luck. When 7:30 rolls around, it's time to take our places at the starting line. I can feel the tension in the air. The marathon attracts more than 50,000 competitors from around the world and weaves through each of New York's five boroughs. The route starts on Staten Island and winds through Brooklyn, Queens, and the Bronx before making a final push down through Manhattan and into Central Park to the finish line. I know this course well since I've raced it twice before. But the surface of the roads can change from year to year, bringing new bumps and potholes to watch for. In past marathons I've gotten flat tires because of the road conditions.

Because there are so many competitors, there are different starting times for different groups. The professional wheelchair racers—about 50 of us in total—are at the front of the pack. Men start first, and then women. We are followed by other professional athletes with disabilities, amateur racers with disabilities, other professional athletes, and finally by the amateur runners. Trying to navigate through 50,000 other racers, especially in racing chairs, is not easy, so I'm glad to be at the front.

Gripping my wheels, I try to focus on the racecourse and visualize each stretch of road, each turn, each hill. In a few minutes I will race in one of the most grueling marathons of the year—26.2 miles across roadways, bridges, and hills, the whole way being watched by thousands of people lined up along the course, and millions more watching on television!

The crowd grows quiet as the seconds on the clock tick down. I stare straight ahead, trying not to look at the other racers, or at the crowds nearby.

"Just relax and breathe!" I say to myself. My mind

How does a racing chair work?

Wheelchair racing has been part of the Paralympics since 1960. Early racing chairs were bulky standard wheelchairs. In the 1970s, athletes started to create streamlined models using lighter metals better suited for racing.

Today's racing chairs typically have aluminum frames, carbon fiber wheels fitted with tubeless rubber tires. The wheels tilt inwards towards the rider so that riders don't bump their arms on the wheels.

The outside of each wheel has a rubber-coated handring. Wearing padded gloves made of rubber and plastic, racers propel and brake by pushing down on the handrings with their hands.

Racers steer using a small u-shaped device connected to the frame on the front wheel. Since it is difficult to push and steer at the same time, a small spring keeps the front wheel aligned while the racer is pushing on the handrings.

counts down the seconds, "...five...four...three...two...one...."

"*Runners on your mark!*"

"CRACK!" A blast from the starting gun, and the men are off. I feel a jolt of adrenaline even though it's not my turn to start. Then two minutes later, "CRACK!" The gun goes off a second time, and the women blast out from the starting line. I'm off!

I push to get ahead of the other racers. My eyes are focused on the crest of the bridge—I have to get over that first rise. To the left of me, the pale purple-blue outline of the skyscrapers of Manhattan peeks through the haze of morning light.

Now I'm over the crest and picking up speed as I head down the other side of the bridge. I'm going too fast.

"Slow down! Slow down!" I think as I brake. On the Brooklyn side, the spectators are cheering. My heart pounds with excitement.

"Just keep calm!" I caution myself.

At the bottom of the hill, the course turns at almost a ninety-degree angle. This isn't a big deal for runners, but for those of us in racing chairs, going too fast around a sharp corner can send us hurtling. At the turn is a huge wall of hay bales, stacked high to catch racers who don't make the turn. Even so, hay isn't the softest cushion. If I hit the wall of hay too fast I could crack the frame or a wheel, or worse, injure

Heading over the Verrazano Bridge.

myself and be unable to continue.

I make the turn safely, veering close to the cheering spectators and onto the streets of Brooklyn. I race along Fourth Avenue through neighborhoods of tiny shops, factories, and low-rise brick row houses. There are no big hills to climb in Brooklyn and Queens, only a few sharp turns to navigate, so I settle into my pace and concentrate on the motion of my arms propelling me along.

People line the streets waving and shouting, and I hear, somewhere in the distance, a band playing. It's like a big street party, but I speed by the crowd, alone in my own little world. I'm in my "zone," concentrating on the road, barely aware of what's going on around me. I feel each breath, each push of my arms, each turn of my wheels.

Heading down the course.

"Pace myself!" I think as I glance down at my Garmin, a small device like a sports watch that is strapped to my chair and tells me my pace and how far I have left to go. If I push too fast here, I'll be too tired for the second half of the race.

My Garmin tracks my speed and distance.

An hour into the race I've reached Mile 15. The Queensboro Bridge and the towers of Manhattan rise in front of me. I speed up as I come onto the incline over the East River. The cold wind off the water hits me. I race across the bridge, descending into midtown Manhattan and onto First Avenue.

"Go! Go! Go!" The cheering behind the barricades on First Avenue hits me with a wall of sound. It's exciting and invigorating to know that all these people have gathered on this cold morning to watch us race—to watch *me* race! My heart pumps even faster.

First Avenue is one very long, slow-rising hill. I need to reset my pace again. All I can think about is that I have another ten miles to go. The climb is exhausting. My arms are feeling stiff and sore.

I head up and into the Bronx and then turn back across a small rusted metal bridge and into Manhattan again for the last big stretch down Fifth Avenue and into Central Park.

I am ahead of the other racers, but I'm not sure by how much. If I look back now, it might cost me valuable seconds. And if I don't watch in front of me, I could hit a rock or pothole in the road that could send me tumbling.

"Keep going!" I repeat over and over.

Racing down Fifth Avenue, I turn into Central Park at 90th Street. I know the hills of the park well. I had trained there earlier in the week and memorized all the dips and turns. Most of the way is slightly downhill, which scares me a little. Because I'm lighter than many of the racers, maintaining control going down a hill has caused me trouble before. Luckily, this hill isn't that steep.

"Just focus," I think again.

"GO, TATYANA, GO!" I hear my name. I wonder if it's my family or friends. I steal a quick glance, but the crowd is a sea of colored parkas. My arms are throbbing now as I pour on the speed for the final blast to the finish line. All I can think about is the pain I'm feeling. My arms are cramping, my stomach's in knots, and my eyes are blurring up from the icy wind.

"Less than one mile to go!" I reassure myself.

I push harder and faster, heading down past the Metropolitan Museum of Art, the boathouse, and then the zoo.

On either side of me, spectators cheer me on as I fly by. Ahead of me, I see the fountain at 59th Street. From there it's a simple quick four blocks along the south edge of the park and back north into the park to the finish line! I am almost there! My mind fills with a dozen thoughts–

"Grand Slam!"

"Focus!"

"Watch the road!"

"FOCUS!"

"Is there anyone behind me?"

"FOCUS!"

"GO, GO, GO!" the crowd chants. The frenzied cheers fill my head and give me a last burst of energy.

I come out from under the trees and turn onto 59th Street. My chair starts to wobble. I try to slow down and steady myself, but it's too late. I cut the turn too tightly! My head hits the pavement hard. My racing chair topples over me. People are running to help. The police try to help me up. I'm shaking.

"Don't touch me!" I shout.

If someone tries to help me get up and going again, there is a chance I could be disqualified. My head is swirling. I'm breathless. My body is vibrating.

What happens if there's a flat tire?

Making sure a racing chair is in tip-top shape is criti- cal to winning. Well before a race begins, riders care- fully check to make sure that the tires are in good shape, there are no cracks in the frame, and no loose bolts in the wheel or gear  mechanism. A loose bolt can be tightened, but a crack in the frame is much more serious. Both rarely happen if the racing chair is checked regularly.

Flat tires are the most common problem and are usually caused by the rough terrain of the roadways. Each athlete carries a spare inflatable tire.

When a tire blows, the rider pulls over to the side of the road. Without getting out of his or her chair, the rider removes the spare tire, switches out the flat, and inflates the tire with a small canister of compressed air. For an athlete who has practiced changing tires this should take no more than a minute. It can often unnerve a racer, especially when it happens in the last minutes of a race. But if the racer keeps cool, it doesn't have to spell disaster!

"Stay calm! Stay calm!" I repeat over and over.

"I am so close! Is the chair all right? Did anyone pass me?" My mind is dizzy with thoughts of what to do.

Pushing my chair and myself back upright, I pray that the wheels didn't crack or the tires haven't blown out. The crowd is silent, holding its breath. I push off.

"Don't look back. Don't look back!" I tell myself. Stopping to see where the other racers are would cost me valuable time. I know a race is often won by a lead of less than the length of a nose—a few tenths of a second. I just need to power through to the finish line. I only have a few more meters to go and can see the blue ribbon at the finish line. It isn't far.

"*Ya sama, ya sama!*—I can do it! I can do it!"

I push harder and harder, not knowing how close anyone is behind me. The finish line is just ahead. Almost there! I feel the slight resistance of the finish line ribbon against my chest. I did it! I've won it again! The Grand Slam!

I collapse back into my chair, my arms pulsing, my shoulder bruised, and try to catch my breath. My body hurts from the race and from the fall, but I am filled with the exhilaration of finishing the marathon, coming in first place, and winning a second Grand Slam. It took every ounce of physical and mental energy I had, but I did it!

I am now an eleven-time gold, silver, and bronze-medal summer Paralympic athlete, a silver-medal winter Paralympic athlete, fifteen-time World Champion—and now, with this race—winner of twelve major world marathons and two Grand Slams.

✶

I am humbled. When I fell down in the race, I could have admitted defeat. I had messed up, but then I remind myself of something I had once heard: Failure is not falling down, but refusing to get up. Much of my life I have fallen down. It sort of comes with the territory of having a disability, but rarely, if ever, have I refused to get up and keep going.

Crossing the finish line!

CHAPTER 2

Beginnings

Y A SAMA!" In Russian, it literally means "I, myself," but it can also be translated as "I can do it" or "I can do it myself."

This is what I say anytime I am faced with a challenge or start to doubt myself. It is an expression I learned as a young child in Russia. I have always believed that I could do anything I set my mind to. Of course that doesn't mean it always comes out exactly the way I hoped, but I am rarely disappointed in the result.

★

I was born in the spring of 1989 in St. Petersburg, Russia.

At the orphanage. My first formal portrait!

I was born with *spina bifida,* a condition that left my spinal cord malformed and my legs without feeling or movement. It must have been heart-breaking news for my young mother when she was told that I was not expected to live more than a few days.

I can imagine the doctors' sad consolation. "We are so sorry...but your baby will not live to see the summer. It will be best for the child if she is placed in the government hospital until then." My mother, like many people in Russia at that time, couldn't afford to care for me properly.

"She will be better there. You should go about your life and place her in God's hands now."

So she reluctantly gave me up to become a ward of the state. As fortune would have it, I didn't die. After several months in the hospital, I was placed in an orphanage.

Baby House #13 was for infants and toddlers up to the age of four. The children were looked after by a staff of women—caregivers who weren't trained doctors or nurses and knew little about how to care for a child like me. I have been told that for the first year of my life, some of them prayed for my suffering to end. But by the end of the first year I was still alive, and while frail and sickly, I gave no signs of withering away.

When I look back now at pictures of the orphanage where I spent my first years, it looks pleasant enough. Baby House #13 is located along a small river in a pretty, older part of St. Petersburg. But as I remember it as a child, the

What is *spina bifida*?

The name spina bifida comes from the Latin language and means "split spine." It is a birth defect in which the backbone (spine) does not close completely around the spinal cord. This can lead to leg and walking problems, as well as issues with other internal organs that are located around the spine. Scientists believe spina bifida may be caused by a combination of genetic and environmental factors.

orphanage was a place of long empty hallways, dim flickering lights, and cold drafty rooms. It was a place filled with the sounds of crying babies and the smell of boiled cabbage and potatoes.

I slept in a room with about a dozen other children, in small beds set up side by side. Each day started with the arrival of the caregivers. The lights would go on. And one by one, each of us was taken to the washroom to be quickly washed with a cold-water hose and then brusquely dressed in coarse cloth diapers and second-hand clothing. We all shared the same clothes, an odd assortment of ill-fitting pants, tights, shirts, and sweaters that might be too small one day and too big the next.

Breakfast was a bowl of porridge. Lunch and dinner consisted most often of a thin pale soup, sometimes with bits of boiled vegetables in it. I don't remember if we ever

had meat. If we did, it was probably just a small portion added to the soup for flavor. The older kids were served soup in dented aluminum and plastic bowls while babies were given bottles to suck on. I often wonder if the babies got the same soup in their bottles instead of proper baby formula. There was never much to eat, but the caregivers probably gave us what they could.

Occasionally, there might be a slice of apple with our porridge. And at other meals some fresh cucumbers, tomatoes, and dense, sour-tasting black bread to soak up the thin soup and help fill our bellies.

Between meals we were put in cribs or on plastic floor mats, where we passed the time sitting, napping, and playing. I use the word "playing" loosely as there wasn't much to play with. Sometimes people donated toys to the orphanage. We got to play with them for a few hours, and then the caregivers would take them and place them high up on a shelf for safekeeping. Once the toys were put away, the caregivers usually forgot to bring them out again. I guess it was because there were so many children and not many toys, that the caregivers wanted to make sure that they weren't broken or worn out from overuse.

Each day was like the last. Each day was spent doing the same things over and over. There were few activities and no classes. The caregivers rarely talked to us except

Baby House #13 in St. Petersburg, Russia.

when they herded us out of our beds, to meals, and then back to bed. Since we were all "babies," there was no reason to engage us in conversation. The only words we learned were from each other, or from listening to the caregivers. Their voices turned to whispers if they became aware of us eavesdropping on them.

At nighttime the orphanage was a terrifying place. As nice or indifferent as the caregivers during the day might be, the people who came to watch over us at night were our nightmares. Grumbling and angry, they would shout at crying babies, as if somehow that would quiet them. They'd also punish anyone who tried to get out of bed for a drink of water or to go to the bathroom. Leaving our beds was forbidden and we had to wait until the caregivers on the day shift got to work.

As I got older I learned the importance of being friendly and polite to the caregivers in the day so they might talk to me, give me an extra piece of black bread at suppertime, or even slip me a rare piece of candy. And I learned to be silent and invisible to those who watched us in the night.

✶

In summer, when the air was warm, some of us might be taken outside to the small yard of hard-packed dirt that surrounded the orphanage. There were no grass or flowers, only a small play area with several large metal playpens

waiting in bed for the day caregivers to come wash and dress me.

where they placed us. A tall wrought-iron fence separated the yard and the orphanage from the street. As there were not many people to care for us, we were often left alone. Sometimes stray dogs stuck their heads through the iron fence, snarling and growling. Occasionally one of the scrawnier dogs would wiggle through the bars and try to climb over into our playpens.

I'm not sure if the dogs would have actually bitten us, but the mere sight of them sent us into a panic of screams and tears until a caregiver came running out of the building with a broom in hand.

"Shoo! Get out of here!" she'd yell, chasing the mangy animal, whacking it hard with the broomstick as it retreated, yelping, back through the fence. The caregiver would try to console us, hurriedly rushing us back inside to the safety of our rooms. That was all I knew about being outside.

Looking out the windows or through the bars of the fence, my world ended at the tops of the buildings across the street and at the far side of the canal. There were no books to read, no television to watch, no Internet to explore. There was no one to teach me, no one to read to me. In my small world, I knew so little. One day was like the next. There were no weekends and no holidays. My days had no names; my hours had no numbers.

✶

As the other babies learned to crawl, I learned to pull myself along on my hands, dragging my limp legs behind me. As they started to walk, I learned to tuck my legs, one over the other, and scoot along the floor, or lift my body up onto my arms and pull myself across the ground.

When I was about five, I discovered that I could walk. But not in the way other kids were walking on their feet. Instead, I'd lift myself up on my arms and swing back repeatedly until I was upside down and balancing myself. Then I'd walk one hand after another.

It seemed natural for me to "walk" like this and more convenient to scoot myself around with my arms. I could

climb onto chairs, tables, and even up
onto shelves to reach the forbidden
toys, or just to gaze out a window.

At first the caregivers scolded
me for all of my moving around. Worried
that I might hurt myself they placed me
back in my pen with a stern "Nyet—No!"
But as I grew, it became easier for me to
slip out of my pen and scoot, climb, and
walk upside down before replying to them
with a triumphant "Ya sama!" Eventually
they let me be.

On one occasion, a man arrived
with a large box that he placed in the
middle of the floor of our play area. All the older children
were summoned to watch as, one by one, their names were
called and they were handed a new pair of shoes. Each child
took the prized gift back to his or her corner to try on. My
name was never called. I pulled myself over to the big box and
pushed myself up onto my hands, peering inside the box. It
was now empty. There were no shoes for me. I couldn't walk,
so I guess they would have been little use to me. But still,
I would have liked to have had a pair of my own.

✱

In the orphanage, where love and attention were rare,
I remember few faces or friends. There were one or two

children whom I played with, but as I grew older, they would leave the orphanage. But there was one person I will always remember: Natalya. She was the director of the orphanage and had watched over me since I was a baby. I felt safe with Natalya. She was my guardian angel, making sure I was taken care of when I was sick and that I had enough to eat.

When I was a bit older, Natalya would let me come and sit in her office while she worked. I would wait patiently outside her door until she noticed me and invited me in.

"Good morning, Tatyana!" she would say cheerfully with a warm smile, looking over her dark-rimmed glasses at me. "Come in, come in!"

I'd pull myself in and climb up onto a chair next to her desk. Behind her a large samovar hissed steam as she poured hot water from it into a teapot and then prepared a small glass of cherry-sweetened tea for me.

"We must find you a home!" Natalya said to me one day. I wasn't sure what she meant. I thought this was my home. I had seen other children leave the orphanage but didn't know where they went. "We must find you a family to adopt you!"

I didn't understand at the time but Natalya was worried for me. I was now five years old and had become too old to live at Baby House #13. I would soon be evaluated by state physicians to determine where I should be sent—either to a state asylum for the sick and incurable, or to an orphanage for older children. If I was sent to the state asylum I would never leave there. If I was placed in another orphanage, there was no telling what it might be like. Many orphanages were far worse than anything I had experienced at Baby House #13. My best chance, as Natalya knew well, was to be adopted by a foreign family, since few Russians adopted children, and even fewer wanted a child with disabilities like me.

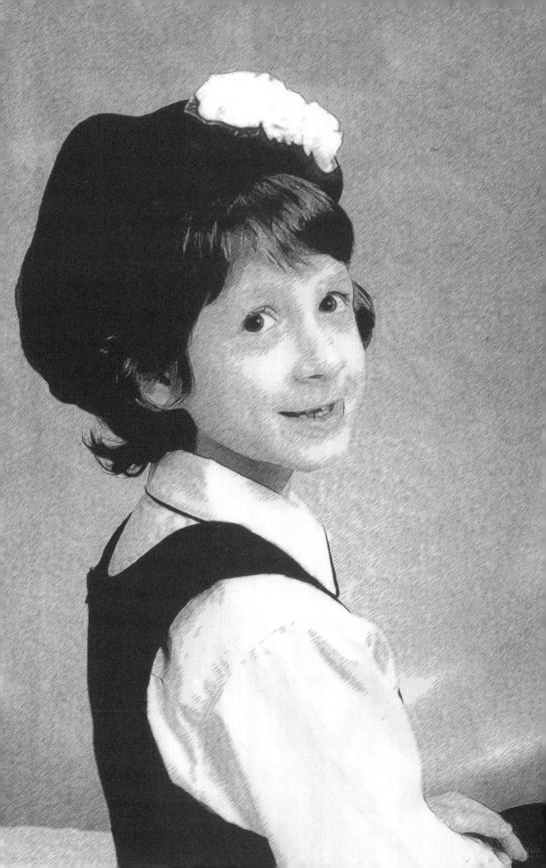

CHAPTER 3

Tetushka

My life changed in the spring of 1994. I remember it was spring because the branches on the trees around the orphanage were turning light green with tiny new leaves. All the windows in the orphanage had been flung wide open to let in the cool breeze. It blew through the rooms and down the hallways, replacing the building's stale air with the fresh fragrance of the river and sprouting leaves.

One of the caregivers was on her knees, bent over a blue plastic bucket, scrubbing away at the floor, back and forth with a hard brush, scrubbing so hard that a small wall of bubbles was growing around her higher and higher.

Me in my finest dress!

As hard as she cleaned the worn yellowed floor tiles, they never looked any brighter to me. The spring air mixed now with the fumes of ammonia and scouring powder.

"We're having visitors today," I thought to myself. They only cleaned like this when we were having visitors.

The newly clean floors were slow to dry in the cold air and made it difficult for me to go anywhere, so I stayed in the playroom, my dress already damp from my morning explorations.

After lunch we were given fresh clothes to put on. They were "dressy" clothes–something we rarely wore. The caregivers did what they could to clean and dress us up to make the best impression on the visitors. For us girls that meant bright-colored dresses with big white and pink bows for our hair. My bow was almost as big as my head!

"*Privet! Privet!*–Greetings! Greetings!" I heard from the front entrance way. A woman had arrived followed by several people carrying boxes with big plastic bags stacked on top. I was excited. This usually meant food and medicine, but best of all–special treats for the children.

They all went upstairs to Natalya's office to talk and have tea and then proceeded to go from room to room, visiting each of the nurseries. I watched from outside in the hallway as they filed into my nursery room. I was peering around the corner, when one of the caregivers stepped in front of me, blocking me from seeing into the room. I don't think they wanted me in there, so I waited behind the corner of the doorway, occasionally poking my head around like a curious mouse.

The woman sat, smiling as the children were brought to her. She would talk to them and give each of them a big hug and some candy. As she looked around the room, she spotted me behind the caregivers who had crowded in the doorway to watch. She smiled, waving and motioning to me to come in. The caregiver in front of me stepped aside. In my best dress and bow, I scooted myself across the floor to her. Greeting me with kind eyes and a smile, she reached out, lifting me onto her lap.

"*Kak vas zovut?*–What's your name?" she asked.

"Tatyana!" I said proudly with a big smile. I had never sat on the lap of a stranger before. She hugged me and pressed her lips to my cheek. The warmth of her skin and a scent of flowers and soap enveloped me. She didn't smell like the orphanage.

"*Tetushka!*" I said to her. Tetushka is a name given as a sign of affection, like calling someone your auntie.

"Tatyana!" she said, pointing to me.

"Tetushka!" pointing to herself.

"*Da!*–Yes!" I said and hugged her again.

She handed me a lollipop.

"*Spasibo!*–Thank you!" I giggled. I don't think I had ever felt quite so happy. I pushed my lips to her cheek and pressed like she had done to mine. She laughed.

"No, no, like this." She pursed her lips against my hand

and made a smacking noise, then pulled away.

"*Poseluy*–Kiss." She pressed her lips to my cheek and made the smacking sound again. I placed my lips to her cheek and pulled away with a light smack.

She hugged me and held me close. I felt her heart beat as I nestled my head against her. I was only in her lap a few minutes before Natalya lifted me up and placed me back on the floor.

"That's enough, little one. There is much to see," she said, indicating to the woman that it was time to visit the rest of the orphanage. Natalya stood up and walked out the door to continue on the tour. The woman stood and looked back at me with one more smile, and with that the other caregivers followed her out. I trailed behind them as they went from room to room, my lollipop tucked safely in my pocket, the feel of her kiss fresh on my cheek.

At the end of the afternoon, the woman gave me another big hug and a kiss. I watched from the top of the stairs as she departed.

✶

The next day, she returned with more gifts for the orphanage and more candy for us kids.

"Tetushka!" I cried out when I saw her coming up the stairs.

"Little Tatyana!" she said smiling and laughing. She handed me a small brown bag.

"This is for you and only you!" she said. Inside was a small stuffed bunny rabbit with big floppy ears and an orange bow around its neck. I lifted it out of the bag, rubbing its furry face against mine. Gifts in the orphanage were normally shared, but this was just for me! I held my new friend in my arms as Tetushka held me in hers.

After she left, Natalya placed a small framed photograph of Tetushka on a shelf in the playroom.

"That's my mother!" I told one of the caregivers.

"No, that is just a nice lady who comes from America," she said sternly.

"No, no! That is my mother!"

"Yes, yes, dreaming. It is good for you to dream..." Her voice trailed off in a way that revealed her cynicism and perhaps her own lack of hopes and dreams. I think she expected me to be sad, but I wasn't listening to her. I wasn't sad. I had seen other children leave the orphanage and knew now that some went to new homes with new parents. I knew this was my chance. I knew that Tetushka would be my mom and that I'd go to live with her. Whenever I walked past the shelf with the photo, I'd hold it in my hands and look into Tetushka's eyes, repeating softly to myself, "This is my mom,

Me and my Tetushka.

this is my mom..."

I later learned that Tetushka was part of an international effort to bring supplies to kids in orphanages and
hospitals across Russia. Over the next year she visited the
orphanage every few months.

On one visit she brought me a wheelchair. I had never
seen such a chair before! It was big and heavy, painted sky
blue, with a black plastic seat, and large spoked wheels, like

the wheels of a bicycle, on each side of the seat. She lifted me up and placed me in the chair, then rolled me back and forth and pushed me down the hall. I laughed and ran my hands over the turning wheels.

"Push, Tatyana, push!" She placed my hands on the wheels and pushed down on them to turn the wheels on the chair. It didn't take me long to figure out how to propel the chair myself, stop it, and turn around. Back and forth I went, over and over.

"Come on, Tatyana, let's go outside!" Tetushka called to me.

I had never been outside the iron fence of the orphanage before. With Tetushka pushing me from behind, we went out to the street and over the small bridge that crossed the river that I had seen from the play yard.

"Ok, Tatyana, let's see how fast you can go!"

We were on a small dead-end street with no cars. The road was smooth. She gave the chair a push, and I grabbed the wheels, spinning them as best I could, faster and faster. I was flying!

"Bystro! Bystro!—Fast! Fast!" she cheered. Buildings sped past in a blur, the wind tickling my face. I let go of the wheels and let the chair carry me. I coasted to a stop, turned around, raced back down to the corner, and turned and raced down again. How wonderful it felt to move with such ease and speed!

✶

One day I went to visit Natalya. Tetushka was sitting in her office.

"Tatyana, would you like to join us for tea?" With a big smile I pulled myself into Natalya's office and up onto a chair. There was a small tray of porcelain teacups. I watched as Natalya poured tea into three of them. One for Tetushka, one for herself, and one for me.

I had never been served tea like this before! I tried to sit up as straight as I could. Natalya lifted her cup to her lips, each time sticking out her little pinky finger as she sipped. I had watched the caregivers on their morning break drinking tea from water glasses and large thick mugs but hadn't seen them ever lift their pinkies.

I carefully lifted my cup and slowly pushed out my pinky, raising the tiny cup to my lips.

"Tatyana, would you like to go live with Tetushka in America?"

"*Da! Da!*—Yes! Yes!"

I had no idea what or where America was. It could have been a house on the next block or on the Moon. But I knew since the first day I met her that Tetushka would be my mother and more than anything that I wanted to be with her.

"Tatyana. Tatyana is such a big name!" Tetushka gestured and stretched out with her hands. "Can I call you Tanushka? Or Tanya?"

I shook my head. I didn't like either of them. Tatyana was my name.

"So what can I call you?" she asked?

"*Dochska*—Daughter," I replied with a hug.

CHAPTER 4

To America

You be a good girl in America!" Natalya said.

Natalya stood in the doorway holding me in her arms. It was my last day at the orphanage. I had said goodbye to the other children and the caregivers, and now it was the last farewell.

"Yes, yes, I promise!" I replied.

She held me and rocked me back and forth silently.

"Okay, little Tatyana, it's time to go!" Natalya placed me in Tetushka's arms.

"Thank you so much," Tetushka said to Natalya, "for everything!"

Me and my mom in Moscow's Red Square.

The driver stored my wheelchair and a small bag of clothes that Natalya had given me for my journey into the trunk of the taxi. Tetushka placed me in the back seat and then slipped in beside me.

I pulled myself up to the window and reached out to wave. The taxi pulled out onto the street. Natalya followed us, waving and dabbing her eyes with a handkerchief as her glasses slipped down cockeyed on her nose.

"Natalya! Natalya!" I cried.

The taxi picked up speed. I pressed my face to the window as Natalya grew smaller and smaller. Then she was gone behind the traffic. I slumped back onto the seat crying. Tetushka pulled me close and held me as I sobbed harder and harder.

"Now, now, Tatyana, everything will be okay," she said, trying to comfort me.

Looking up, all I could see now were the tops of the gray buildings passing by and the dull evening sky. I had no idea where I was going. I pressed my face into the darkness of Tetushka's coat as she stroked my hair.

✳

When I woke we were pulling into the train station. Tetushka placed me in the wheelchair. I was exhausted from so much crying, but the excitement and activity of the train station distracted me from my sadness. People were rushing everywhere. Porters hurried with bags toward the long dark trains that billowed out clouds of steam across the station.

"*Moskva Ekspress, trek dvadtsat' dva!* Moscow Express train, track twenty-two," a deep voice blasted out of the loudspeaker.

We pressed through the crowd to the Moscow-bound train and boarded.

"This looks like our compartment here." Tetushka studied our tickets and then checked the numbers on the door. The compartment was small with two worn leather seats that ran it's length, facing each other. She placed me on one of the seats by the window. The porter slid in our luggage and the wheelchair. The cabin was a sleeping car, so the benches folded out into beds. Tetushka opened a bed and placed her luggage on it.

"Be careful, Tatyana!"

I pulled myself up to the open window to look out. A whistle sounded. The train lurched back and forward, and then we were off through a cloud of steam into the night. The lights of the city sped by, growing fewer and fewer. Soon we were passing through the countryside, and I watched the sky grow dark.

"*Bilety, pozhaluysta!*—Tickets, please!" Tetushka pulled out the tickets and handed them to the conductor, then closed the door and locked it. The rocking of the train made me drowsy. Tetushka placed me on the empty bed and lay down next to me to sleep.

"Tetushka, what this—America?" I asked in the few

words of English that I knew.

"Well, Tatyana, America is a big country, with lots of things to do, and many people, and much food..." Most of her words I didn't understand. Occasionally she said something I recognized, and I'd repeat the word over and over in my head. I drifted into sleep, comforted by her lilting voice and the motion of the train as it rocked and clacked in rhythm to her lullaby of words about America.

✶

The next morning, I was no longer sad. A new day was starting. I was no longer in the arms of Tetushka, I was in the arms of my mother.

I crawled back to the window and for several hours watched as the fields and forests flew by. Bare trees and roads disappeared into a grey fog. The air smelled of damp smoke. After a while the fields became dotted with buildings. Then more buildings appeared until the open fields were gone, replaced with row after row of dark buildings. More buildings than I had ever seen before stretched as far as I could see. The sun was coming up over the rooftops.

We pulled into the station, and the train lurched to a stop. My mother piled our luggage on the wheelchair and picked me up in her arms. On the train platform, someone was waving at us.

"*Dobroye utro!*–Good morning!" A young Russian couple approached us, waving and smiling,

"Hello!" Mom greeted them and turned to me. "Tatyana, this is Masha and Pasha. They will be helping us while we are here in Moscow."

I had not met many young men before. Pasha looked so serious, until his face lit up in a big smile.

"Welcome, little one!" Pasha said cheerfully as he stooped over to shake my hand.

Masha looked like an angel. Her eyes twinkled like stars, and her skin was as pale as Natalya's porcelain teacups.

My mom chatted and laughed with Masha and Pasha as they led us to a small black sedan parked at the front of the train station.

The fog lifted as we drove through the streets of Moscow. The darkened structures I had seen from the train were now coming alive with activity, and the sidewalks began to fill with people. Our car pulled up to a large building. Pasha lifted me out and carried me down the long red carpet stretching from the sidewalk to the front door.

Inside, the bright lights inside hurt my eyes. When I focused I could see large white marble columns capped by tall golden lamps. The walls and ceilings sparkled and glittered. I had been carried into a new world.

"Is this America?" I asked.

Pasha laughed, "No little one! This is Moscow!" he said proudly.

✳

After we had checked into the hotel, we spent the rest of the morning visiting various government offices getting all the proper paperwork so I could leave Russia.

As we went through the streets of Moscow, people stared at me. I don't think they had ever seen a little girl in a wheelchair. Most children like me were kept in hospitals and homes and didn't go outside often. I suppose they thought we were tourists because we were all smiles and giggles while everyone else looked so serious and grim.

There was so much to see! Ice cream vendors and street carts full of flowers and candy. A man was playing a balalaika, which is sort of like a Russian banjo. Pasha placed something in the hat on the ground in front of him. The musician smiled and nodded at us.

"You see, little one, these are rubles—Russian money. I gave the man some rubles so he'll play a song for us."

I had never seen money before. And I had never heard such beautiful music!

Then from another man, Pasha traded his rubles for a balloon for me. I could go on and on about all the things that we did. In that one afternoon, I had my first taste of ice cream, soda pop, and chocolate! We explored store after store selling things I had never imagined.

with Pasha and Masha on my first shopping trip.

One sold all sorts of small curios—snow globes with tiny scenes of Moscow, carved wooden animals, china figurines, colorful scarves, glass paperweights, gilded framed portraits of important-looking people. Then my mother found a shelf of small wooden dolls.

"Open it up!" she said, handing one of the dolls to me.

I sat and stared at the pretty doll painted in red and gold to look like a Russian babushka. Masha reached over and neatly twisted off the top of the doll. Inside was another doll! Laughing at my surprise, she pulled out the second one. Then she twisted the top off that doll and inside was another doll! And then another until there were five dolls in all. I laughed with delight at the dolls spread out on my lap, twisting the smallest and hoping for yet another one inside. Mom went back into the store to get several more.

"No, no, one is enough!" I said, not knowing what I would do with so many dolls!

"No, these are gifts for your new family in America," Mom replied. My new family? I was just getting used to the idea of my new mom. It was a gift I could barely imagine.

✶

The next morning, my mother and I said goodbye to Masha and Pasha, and we boarded an airplane to America.

Pasha had explained to me how the plane flies through the sky and would take us across a big ocean to America and my new home. Flying in a plane, the ocean, America. I didn't understand exactly what any of these words meant, except that it was another new experience.

Mom placed me in my seat on the plane, buckled me in, and tucked a blanket around me.

"Now, Tatyana, you go to sleep. We have a long journey ahead of us!" she whispered to me, trying to calm me down. But I was excited and restless. I was beginning to like adventures.

After the plane took off, I slipped out of my seat to explore the cabin, scooting up and down the aisles, again and again, introducing myself to the flight attendants who gave me cookies and soda, and the passengers who eyed me and smiled as I passed by their seats.

Finally exhausted from my explorations, I returned to my seat and fell asleep. As the sun came up, I scrambled onto my mother's lap and gazed out at the clouds, the far curved horizon of the earth, and the dark blue ocean below.

Up until that moment, all that I had ever known of the world was what I could see through the iron gates of the orphanage in St. Petersburg. Now, the more I saw, the bigger the world became.

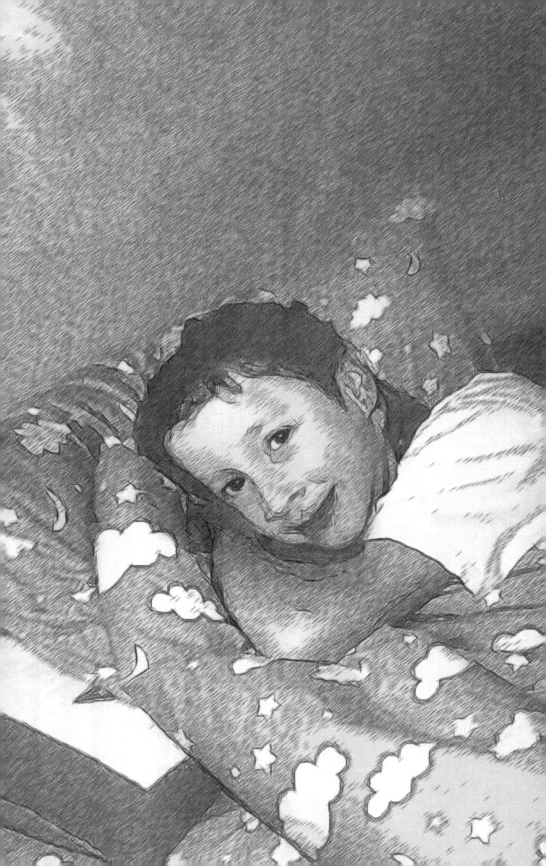

CHAPTER 5

Home

Imagine waking up on Christmas morning, waiting to see what Santa Claus has brought you. Now, multiply that feeling one hundred times. That was how I felt on the first morning in my new home in a small town halfway between Baltimore and the capital of my new country, Washington, D.C.

I lay in bed hugging my pillow, not wanting to open my eyes to the new world that surrounded me. My pillow smelled like springtime, and through the open window I could hear the rustling of leaves. Birds woke me with loud chatter and then lulled me back to sleep with soft cooing.

At the orphanage I wasn't allowed out of bed until

In my new home!

the caregivers came to clean and dress me. Now I waited anxiously in my new bed for my first day in America to begin.

"Good morning!" came a soft voice as the door opened. It was my mother greeting me with a big smile, a hug, and a kiss on my forehead.

"Good morning, Mommy!" This was no longer my Tetushka, this was my mother!

"Tatyana, would you like a bath before breakfast?"

"Da—Yes," I replied hesitantly. I didn't really understand what she was asking. My English wasn't very good, and I didn't remember ever having a bath. In Russia, the caregivers washed me quickly with a splash of cold water and a rough soapy rag.

Mom disappeared into the bathroom. I heard the sound of running water. And then I was sitting in a tub surrounded by mounds of warm soapy bubbles that smelled of flowers and little floating boats and ducks to play with. After the bath, Mom dried me with soft towels. Pressing my face into one, I was filled with the smell of a world clean and new.

At breakfast, instead of the gray porridge that I used to eat, there were tiny boxes covered with colorful drawings of animals and people. Each box contained a different breakfast cereal. One tasted like chocolate, another like fruit, and another was covered in a white powdery sugar.

There was also fresh fruit, but instead of a single slice of an apple, there was a bowl full of apples, oranges, and bananas, along with yogurt, toast, jam, and juice. It was hard to believe it was all for me!

"Tatyana, go look outside!" Mom said, pointing to the open kitchen door. I climbed down from my chair and scooted over to the doorway. I could hear a racket of noise. Across the yard, a large group of people had gathered along the road that ran behind the house.

Mom followed me outside and, placing me in my wheelchair, pushed me up to the edge of the yard and through the crowd. Down the road, people were running towards us. On both sides of the road the crowd was cheering and clapping for the runners as they got closer.

I cheered too as they ran by. Mom hooked up a garden hose, and we sprayed the heated runners who ran close to us. I held up my hand like I saw other people doing.

"High five!" yelled one of the runners as he approached, bowing down to slap my hand.

Looking back now as a professional athlete, I often wonder if I just imagined seeing a race on my first day in America. But I've been assured by my mom and others who were there that it did, in fact, occur. It was just one of the many fantastical events that have filled my life.

$$\star$$

The next morning after breakfast, again I heard sounds coming from outside. This time it was from the front of the house and sounded like children. But instead of cheering, it was laughing and singing.

"*Strawberry shortcake, huckleberry pie...*"

I pulled myself up to the front window and saw three girls on the sidewalk in front of the house. Two of them were swinging a rope in big circles while the third hopped over it as it slapped the ground.

"*Pozhaluysta*—Please?" I asked, pointing out the window.

"Tatyana, you can't..." Mom stopped herself in mid-sentence. Then she smiled. "Sure! Why don't you go out and introduce yourself."

I scooted out the front door and over to the girls. They looked at me strangely at first. I couldn't walk, and I spoke in an odd language, but I could do something they couldn't. I pointed at the rope and back to myself. By this time they had stopped spinning the rope, so I jumped into the middle and flipped upside down and balanced myself on my hands. It took a few tries to get it right, but before long, they were spinning and singing and I was jumping, from one hand to another, over the rope.

✦

Every day brought more adventures. I explored my new home, looking into rooms, opening cabinets and drawers and closets. The refrigerator fascinated me with its icy-cold air and stacks upon stacks of food, jars of pickles, cheeses, meats, and vegetables.

Heading out for a new adventure!

I flipped through magazines and books, looking at pictures of people, places, and things that were all new to me. I didn't understand the words—but even if they had been in Russian I wouldn't have been able to read any of it, as I hadn't been taught to read or write in any language.

I watched television not knowing what I was seeing or hearing. Every once in a while I'd hear a familiar-sounding word and repeat it to myself over and over.

Outside, when my mom worked in the garden, I played with the garden hose, or looked under stones at the small insects and worms that hid there, or picked the small yellow flowers that grew in the grass.

"What is that?" I asked.

"A ladybug," Mom replied.

"What is that?"

"That is a dandelion."

"What is that?"

"That is an oak tree."

Every answer brought another question from me.

"What is that?"

"That's where we get our mail. It's called a mailbox."

"What's mail?"

"It is how we get letters from our friends."

"What are letters?"

On and on I asked questions, trying to understand all that was around me. I was curious about everything! I had come from a world that was so very small, where every day I did so very little. Now each day was bursting with new things to see, hear, touch, taste, and smell. It was all so exciting!

✶

Tatyana, how would you like to have a birthday party?" my mom asked me one day.

"Yes, Mommy!" I replied, although I had no idea what a birthday party was. My real birthday had been in the spring, but Mom thought that it would be a good way to introduce me to my new home.

"We can invite over all the neighbors and your new relatives."

We put crepe paper streamers and balloons around the living room, and Mom baked a cake covered in pink icing and candles.

Everyone arrived with packages wrapped in bright paper and ribbons.

We all sat around the dining room table. Mom brought out the cake with six lighted candles on top and set it down in front of me as everyone sang:

"*Happy birthday to you, happy birthday to you! Happy birthday, Tatyana, happy birthday to you!*"

"Now, close your eyes and make a wish, then blow out the candles. If you can blow out all the candles at once, your wish will come true!"

I didn't wish for anything. I couldn't possibly imagine wanting anything more than what I had now!

I had never had cake like this. It tasted of strawberries, and the frosting was sweet and fluffy.

Everyone was chatting and asking me questions.

"How do you like the cake?"

"How do you like your new home?"

"How do you like America?"

"Very nice, all very nice!" I replied, smiling and looking around the table at all the people who had come to celebrate with me.

"What you name?" I asked the girl sitting next to me.

"Jessi McFadden."

"Oh! My name McFadden too!" I responded excitedly.

"What you name?"

"Chelsea McFadden."

"I McFadden too!" I replied in surprise.

"What you name?"

"I'm Grandpa McFadden, but you can call me Grandpa."

"I McFadden too!" I replied again in total amazement.

I looked around the table, asking each person the same question. One by one, almost everyone was named McFadden!

"What an amazing coincidence!" I thought to myself. "Or maybe it's a common name in America."

Suddenly, I realized, as if this had been my birthday wish, that all of these people were my family!

"Open the presents, Tatyana!" Someone motioned to the pile of pretty packages. Everyone gathered around to watch me. I held the first package in my hands, inspecting the beautiful wrapping paper and ribbons.

"Oh!" I exclaimed and neatly untied the ribbon and un-wrapped the package, inspecting the box as I turned it around.

"So very pretty!" I said, carefully opening the box and taking out the pretty doll inside. I looked at it closely.

"Ah, so nice!" I said and then placed the doll back in its box, setting it to the side. Then I opened the next package, again examining the wrapping paper and ribbons, the box, and then the object contained inside, neatly placing it beside me. With each package, I would repeat the process, not stopping to play with any of the contents.

"Why don't you play with your new toys?" Mom asked after the party was over. "All these gifts are for you."

I hadn't thought of this! I had only ever received one gift before and that was the stuffed toy rabbit that Mom had given me in Russia. I couldn't imagine that all these things were for me!

✶

Shortly after my birthday party, Mom took me to the mall to shop for new clothes. I only had a couple of dresses that Mom had bought me before we left Russia, besides the clothes that I had from the orphanage.

"How do you like this one, Tatyana?" Mom asked, pulling a dress out and holding it up in front of me. I looked into the mirror, smiled, and nodded as she placed it in our shopping basket along with other new dresses, tights, and socks. When we got home Mom placed the bright new clothes in the closet in my bedroom, which now was filled with stuffed animals and toys from my birthday party. "Look, Tatyana, six new dresses for you! Which one do you want to wear first?" she said in a pleased voice.

"Too much! Too much!" I protested.

So many things I had never seen. So many things I had never done. It was all so exciting, but also so exhausting.

CHAPTER 6

Swimming Lessons

My first summer in America was a time of discovery and making new friends. A little girl in our neighborhood had also been adopted from an orphanage in Russia. Her name was Mara, and she had two American brothers, Josh and Adam. Mara and I were about the same age, but because of being around her brothers, she was learning English faster than I was. So she often translated words and explained things that were totally new and strange to me. For anyone watching the four of us play together, we must have seemed an odd group, flipping back and forth from English to Russian between our giggles and laughter.

I spent many days with Mara and her brothers in our suburban Maryland neighborhood. I learned all about America from Adam and Josh and compared notes with Mara about

Mara, me, Adam, and Josh.

our new lives. We watched cartoons together and played hide-n-seek, croquet, and chutes and ladders. Mom bought a wading pool for me, and the four of us spent the hot summer days splashing around in the cool clear water. I loved the feeling of water around me and could spend hours just floating and looking up at the clouds in the sky.

Mara and her brothers talked about going swimming and trips to the beach. But I had never learned how to swim, so Mom thought I should take swimming lessons. Besides the fact that I loved to play in the water, she also believed it might make me stronger and healthier.

She called local swim clubs and instructors, but one by one, they all turned us away.

"Impossible!" they said. "She can't even walk; how can she possibly swim!"

One day Mom had an idea.

"Hello? I understand that you are the best swimming instructor in town. Can you teach anyone to swim?"

"Of course! I can teach any child to swim!" the woman replied in a self-assured tone.

"Perhaps you could teach my little girl? She isn't very good with her legs..." Mom made no mention that I couldn't walk.

"Yes, yes. Of course! Not a problem!"

The next day Mom and I arrived at the local swimming pool to meet my new swim instructor. When the instructor saw me in a wheelchair, her face dropped and then tightened

Me and Mara.

in a look of embarrassment.

"My apologies. I didn't know. I'm so sorry, but I can't teach her," she said uncomfortably, "I mean, she can't walk..."

"What does walking have to do with swimming?" Mom asked.

"But..." the woman started to respond.

"Tell you what, I will pay you for four lessons," Mom said, looking down at me, hoping the money and my eager smile were enough to convince her. "Try it for a couple of lessons and if you still don't want to teach Tatyana to swim, then you can keep the rest of the money!"

The woman was quiet for a moment, sizing me up. "Well, okay," she agreed reluctantly. "Tatyana, would you like to get into the water?" She asked delicately as if she was concerned she might upset me.

"*Ya sama!*" I announced enthusiastically. Already dressed in a bathing suit, I quickly wheeled myself over to the pool and plopped down to the edge. Without a moment's hesitation I threw myself into the crystal blue water. I wasn't scared at all. I laughed and pushed myself away from the edge, splashing and swinging my arms, and then sunk like a rock. The instructor fished me out. I was all smiles.

The woman looked over at my mom in surprise. Most young children she coached were usually afraid of the water the first time they got into a pool, gingerly dipping one toe in, slowly backing themselves down the ladder and into the pool—but not me! I took to the water like a goldfish.

Not only did I complete my first four lessons, but I went back every weekend for the rest of the summer!

CHAPTER 7

School Days

A few weeks after I arrived in America Mom took me to visit the nearby elementary school to get me acquainted with it. It was early morning, and the school day was beginning. We pulled up to the large red brick school building. There were lots of kids gathered around the front entrance, and I began to shake.

"Tatyana, everything will be alright." Mom tried to comfort me as I watched all the kids heading into the school.

"Please, Mommy, don't leave me here," I pleaded.

It took a while for Mom to figure out that I thought she was taking me back to an orphanage. I hadn't seen so

On my way to school.

many children in one place since I had left Baby House #13.

We returned later on the same afternoon, as school was letting out.

"Look, Tatyana. See all the children? They're going home to their families."

Kids were streaming out of the building, running, laughing, and hugging their parents.

We went inside and down the clean, brightly lit hallways, peering into rooms filled with small wooden desks. Toys and books lined the shelves. Pictures and maps covered the walls. I was still a little worried, but it didn't feel like an orphanage, so maybe it wouldn't be so bad.

✶

By autumn, so much had changed. I was more comfortable in my new home and had made some new friends in the neighborhood during the summer. They told me all about school. I was now excited about going there and the possibility of making more friends.

On the first day of first grade, Mom came with me.

"This is Miss Sammons. Tatyana, can you say hello?"

Miss Sammons smiled. "Hello, Tatyana!"

"Hello!" I replied, looking around the room. Kids my age were filing into the classroom. Some stared. Some smiled. Some ran past me and into their seats. I sat in the back of the class at a large table, where I could easily sit in my wheelchair. I liked that I could look across the classroom and watch the other kids.

Each morning started with the Pledge of Allegiance. Everyone stood next to their desks and crossed their hands over their hearts. I would wheel my chair around to the front of my table and face the flag, place my hand on my chest, and follow along.

"Iplegallegianssa..." I mumbled, each day picking up one or two more words from the Pledge.

✳

Miss Sammons taught us to read and write. We sang songs, colored, and finger-painted. All these activities came easily to the other kids, but often boggled me. I could barely hold a pencil or crayon in my hand and had only just learned to write my name. I couldn't tell time on a clock. I didn't know how to cut with scissors.

Once a week a special teacher came in to help me speak better English. She showed me flash cards with pictures of common, everyday objects.

"A is for Apple, B is for Banana, C is for Cat, D is for Dog. Now repeat after me," she instructed.

I was easily confused. Only a few months before, apples and bananas were anything but common to me; and as for cats and dogs, all I knew were the mangy mutts that scared me at the orphanage.

"Okay, class, can anyone tell me about Washington, D.C.?" Miss Sammons asked.

"That is where the president lives!" someone shouted.

"In the White House," another added.

"And why is it important?"

"It's the capital of our country!" one kid answered.

"And don't forget small letters too!" I blurted out, proudly trying to participate. But I had confused the nation's capital with capital letters. I was still learning.

✶

At recess, we all went out to play in the school yard. There was a blacktop for jumping rope, foursquare, and hopscotch, and at the far end a playground with a jungle gym and swings. Not knowing anybody to play with, I headed for the jungle gym, pulling myself up onto the bars and climbing around like a little monkey. After a while, I plopped myself into a swing.

"Hi, what you doing?" asked a sandy-haired girl, staring inquisitively at me and smiling.

I was trying to push myself back and forth on the swing, but mostly I was twisting around a lot. Not having any control of my legs made it hard to swing properly.

"Hello!" I said and smiled back as I rocked and twisted.

"Need help with that? Lemme help." She stepped behind me and gave me a gentle push.

She kept pushing until I had enough momentum to rock myself and really get swinging. Then she jumped onto the swing next to me and began to swing until we were both

On the playground.

laughing and screaming, going higher and higher.

"Tatyana, be careful! Come down off of there!

It was the playground monitor, a plump lady who made sure nobody hurt themselves or was roughhousing during recess.

"You two should know better!" she scolded.

We slowed to a stop, and I pulled myself back into my wheelchair as the bell rang.

"Sorry!" we both said.

We headed back to class. I didn't like to cause problems with the teachers, but we really weren't doing anything wrong I thought.

"I'm Kesshi," the girl said with a smile as we went back to our desks.

It was hard to pay attention in class that afternoon. The feeling of flying excited me. I wanted to sneak back out and try and push myself even higher on the swings!

Kesshi and I continued to meet at recess to play. I continued to disregard the playground monitor's warning and scrambled around on the playground equipment. After many days of chasing and scolding me, the monitor reported me to the school principal, who called my mom.

"Ms. McFadden, we're worried about your daughter!" the principal said with concern. "She keeps wanting to climb up the equipment on the playground."

"Yes, and is there something wrong with that?" Mom replied matter-of-factly.

"Well, she shouldn't..."

"Really? And why is that?"

"Well, something might happen," she replied.

"I'm sorry, but I don't see the problem if Tatyana wants to play on the playground."

"But, Ms. McFadden, she might hurt herself!"

"Yes, perhaps she might. But what about the other children? They might fall and hurt themselves too, right?"

"But..." the principal paused.

"Look, she has the same right to hurt herself as anyone else," Mom explained. "Of course I don't want her to get hurt, but I do want her to be treated just like any other child."

In the end the principal agreed to let me play where

I wanted. Kesshi became my new best friend. She would come over to play after school, and we continued our antics on the small plastic playset in the backyard. Kesshi liked to get on the ground and move the way I did, dragging herself around the yard and in the house. Sometimes I'd climb onto the kitchen counter to get to the high shelf where the cookie jar was kept, which was something Kesshi couldn't do, even standing up.

CHAPTER 8

New Shoes

There were many visits to doctors during my first year in my new home. Besides not being able to walk, the doctors said I was too thin and pale. Except for right after I was born, I had never been to see a doctor before. There were no medical records for me from Russia.

At the Shriners Hospital in Philadelphia, the doctors examined my legs, which had become bent and stiff. They explained that I would never be able to walk, but thought I might be more comfortable if my legs were straightened and I was able to bend them.

I can only assume I was an unusual patient because

Taking charge of my x-rays.

after several visits and many tests and x-rays, I was brought into an auditorium by my doctor and presented to a large group of doctors and students. I was placed on the examining table facing my audience. I wasn't used to so much attention!

Clearing his voice, he preceded to talk about me:

"THE patient suffers from acute muscular atrophy caused by spina bifida."

"THE patient has had no physical therapy at all in the last six years, and it is questionable if THE patient has had any major medical treatment at all in that time."

"THE patient this..., THE patient that..." he continued lecturing. My mom stood beside me, getting annoyed as he talked about me like I was a lab rat, but I sat there smiling and basking in the limelight.

"So it is MY opinion," he concluded, "that we should operate on the patient and that the operation could possibly improve the patient's condition. Does that meet with your approval, Ms. McFadden?" the doctor asked, turning his head to look at my mom.

"Tatyana, would you like to have an operation to straighten your legs?" Mom asked me politely. "It will hurt for a while, but it is better for you."

I looked around the room. Everyone was staring at me.

"Well..." I thought, scratching my chin, "will I be able to wear shoes?"

"Yes, young lady, if you wish," the doctor replied.

"If you get this operation, I will buy you a pair of shoes," Mom promised.

I had never worn shoes. It was too difficult to get shoes on my feet because my ankles didn't bend the way most kids' feet do.

"Can I have pink shoes?"

My mom smiled. "Anything you like!"

I hesitated a moment. My audience was silent, on the edge of their seats waiting for my reply.

"Well then, yes, I think I would like to have the operation!" I said in my best English. There were chuckles from the audience. The doctor looked at me with a slightly perplexed look on his face and then smiled.

I remember little about the operation except that when I woke I was in a cast that went from my waist to my toes.

After six weeks the cast came off, and my legs dangled in front of me like other kids.

"I'm long!" I announced, and my mom laughed.

I couldn't walk upside down anymore now that my legs were no longer bent tightly beneath me. But having straight legs made it easier to sit up straight and lie down—and wear my new pink shoes.

Besides my shiny pink patent leather shoes,

which I only wore on special occasions, I also had a pair of white sneakers that I wore when I put on my new metal leg braces. The braces ran from the bottom of my feet and up beside my legs, hips, and torso, held in place by thick padded belts strapped tight against my body.

With my new leg braces on, I started physical therapy every day to help learn how to walk in them. Using a metal frame that I placed in front of me to steady myself, I would lean forward and drag myself slightly, then push out the frame again and drag myself forward.

The braces didn't bend much. If I wanted to sit down, I'd have to loosen the hinges on the braces at the knees and waist until I could bend them enough for me to fall back into a chair.

It was fun seeing the world standing up tall like everyone else. I could reach light switches and open doors more easily than ever before. But my legs didn't get any stronger, and it was tiring pulling myself around. The biggest disappointment for me was that it was slow getting around in the braces. I missed the speed of the wheelchair, and it was difficult to keep up with my friends.

Scooting, climbing, and using my wheelchair had worked pretty well for me before, so after a year of using the braces, I gave them up.

Trying out my new braces.

CHAPTER 9

Just Like the Other Kids

I do not consider myself "wheelchair bound." For the first six years of my life I didn't even know wheelchairs existed. I was perfectly happy scooting around on my hands. But from the first moment I took a ride in the wheelchair Mom brought to the orphanage for me, I fell in love with it. I loved the ease with which I could move around, but more than that, I loved the feeling of speed. It was like having wings!

Mom bought me my own kid-sized wheelchair right after I came to America. It was shiny pink, very light, and easy to manage. I imagine I felt about it the way other kids feel about getting their first bicycle. I had a little pack on

Me with my favorite counselor, Applebee, at Girl Scout camp.

the back to put my things in, which I covered in stickers. I practiced wheeling it around the house, down the driveway and out onto the sidewalk, learning how to turn, go fast, and stop.

It was difficult for me to go up over curbs and big bumps because of the safety blocks on the backs of the wheels. They were meant to stop me from toppling over backwards, but instead they made it harder to get around, so Mom took them off.

Mom also took off the seat belt. I know this might not sound very smart or safe, but I spent a lot of time around swimming pools, and she worried that if I accidentally fell in, the chair might pull me to the bottom.

At school, some of my teachers didn't approve of removing these "safety" features. It was an ongoing struggle to convince them I wouldn't hurt myself if I fell out of my chair, or if I did anything that involved not being in my wheelchair.

✶

The summer after first grade, Mom got me involved in more sports activities besides swimming. I tried horseback riding, rock climbing, trampoline, and tumbling. I would try just about anything. I swung from ropes, climbed up rock walls, bounced along on a raft behind a motorboat, and rode on a jet-ski. I even swam with dolphins!

Swimming with dolphins.

Riding the waves!

I also went to Camp Potomac Woods, a Girl Scout camp, tucked in the hills of northern Virginia. Mom was worried that it might not be very wheelchair friendly. And I was a bit afraid of going on my first trip alone, especially when I got to camp and saw so many other little girls without their parents. Like my first visit to school, it reminded me of the orphanage.

But it didn't take long for me to figure out that the camp was nothing like the orphanage. There was so much to do—art and crafts, sing-alongs, nature walks, and making S'mores around a campfire.

And despite being in the middle of the woods, not being able to walk just wasn't a big problem. There were ramps leading into most of the cabins. If there was somewhere in the camp that I couldn't get to by wheelchair, the counselors let me ride there in the camp's golf cart. And if there were hikes through the woods, one of the camp counselors would carry me piggyback. I was just one more kid in the camp!

My favorite activity was swimming. I was faster in the water than most of the other girls and usually beat them when we raced. It was my first taste of competing in a sport, and I liked it!

✶

After my busy summer, I was excited to get back to school and see my friends. I loved school but when it came to any physical activities, my teachers treated me as if I was a delicate little flower. I was often left to sit in my wheelchair on the sidelines while the other kids played kickball, basketball, volleyball, and other sports. Sometimes the teacher gave me a ball or a balloon to hold to keep me occupied.

Mom stepped in once again. "She just wants to play with everyone else," she pleaded with the gym teacher. He gestured to the long rope dangling from the ceiling and the kids struggling to pull themselves up. It seemed clear that it took a lot of strength and coordination, as well as the use of both arms and legs, to climb the rope.

"And you think she can climb that?"

"I don't know, but at least let her try it first before you dismiss her." Mom insisted.

Mom looked at me and pointed to the ropes. "Tatyana... *up, up?*"

I rolled my wheelchair over to the rope, grabbed the bottom of it, and with my legs dangling beneath me, pulled myself right up to the top.

"Okay, Mommy?" I yelled down.

The gym teacher was dumbfounded, but all the kids cheered and clapped for me. Mom smiled proudly. After that I was included in most of the gym activities, and the kids started to want me on their teams. I think they figured out quickly that being different didn't mean I couldn't do something. It just meant I had to do it in my own way.

CHAPTER 10

The Blazers

The thing about having a *dis*-ability is that people tend to think of what you *can't* do.

"Oh, she *can't* walk."

"She *can't* stand up."

"She *can't* play on the swings."

Once the list of "can'ts" gets going, it's hard to stop it! Soon no one sees what you *can* do.

Mom was determined that I not be defined by what I couldn't do and continued her hunt for physical activities to get me involved in. On one Saturday morning, Mom took me to visit a sports club near our house.

Saturday morning track practice.

"Hello!" a man greeted us. "You must be Tatyana. I'm Coach Herman. Welcome to the Bennett Blazers!"

I didn't really hear him. I was too busy staring. I had never seen so many kids in wheelchairs before, at least a couple dozen kids–all playing basketball!

"Tatyana, perhaps you would like to play a bit? Hey, Josh!" he called to one of the kids. "This is Tatyana. Would you take her over to the juniors and introduce her?"

"Sure! Hey, Tatyana, nice to meet you!" Josh George was a few years older than me with a friendly face surrounded by a tumble of curls. He started bouncing a basketball as we wheeled over to a bunch of kids.

"Hey, everyone, this is Tatyana. She's going to be practicing with us. Tatyana, ever played basketball before?"

"Of course!" I said enthusiastically. I never had, but I didn't want to sound like I didn't know what I was doing.

Josh tossed me the ball. I tried dribbling it a couple times before it hit one of my wheels and went bouncing away.

Somebody threw another ball over to me, and I tried to shoot it into the basketball hoop. I tried again and missed miserably. I know I didn't impress anyone, but no one seemed to care. Everyone was too busy having fun.

For the next few years, most of my weekends were spent with the Blazers. We always started with a swim in the pool. It was only a three-lane pool, and there was always a crazy pile-up of kids as we raced across the pool and back.

It was cold and fun, and I could have stayed in there playing all day. Depending on the season, we played basketball or ice hockey, or raced on the track and practiced field events like throwing a javelin. At the end of each season we competed in tournaments specifically for kids with disabilities. We traveled to Virginia, Pennsylvania, and even as far north as Massachusetts.

I loved competitive sports and became pretty good at basketball. I was faster and out-maneuvered kids a lot older than me. That was the great thing about the Bennett Blazers—age didn't matter. Younger kids played against older kids, boys competed with girls. It helped the younger kids get better and become more confident in themselves and their abilities.

Me and Josh George, far left, with friends on the court.

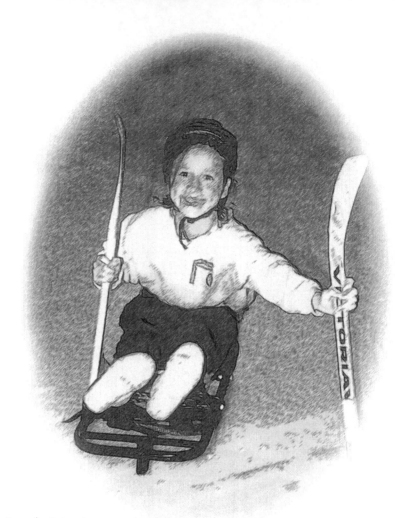

Playing sled hockey.

In the winter we switched to sled hockey, which I absolutely loved. In sled hockey, each player is strapped into a small metal frame mounted on two skate blades. We push ourselves around on the ice using short poles. Like in basketball, I was fast and good at maneuvering around the ice. I was especially good at checking, which is when you drive yourself into your opponent using your upper body and shoulders in order to get the hockey puck away from them. With the Blazers, no one asked me to sit on the sidelines or stay in my chair. I was encouraged and taught and trained to use my body.

Spring was for track-and-field events. Besides wheelchair racing, we completed in discus, shot put, and javelin. On the track, I raced in my everyday wheelchair for the first year. I was faster than most of the kids my own age, so I often practiced with Josh and the older kids. It would have been hard to imagine then that both Josh and I would one day be competing in the Paralympics together!

The following year Josh gave me his old racing chair. It was much sleeker and lighter than my wheelchair. The more I trained, the more my upper body developed muscles. My growing strength and athletic abilities gave me a newfound confidence. Over the next few years, I won quite a few track-and-field medals. I knew I would never be left sitting on the sidelines again.

In the summer of 2002, when I was thirteen, I won the 100-meter sprint at the Junior National Championships and broke the world record for my age group. The officials at the track meets were impressed with me and encouraged Mom to start thinking about focusing more on my racing and to get some professional training for me. But Mom really wanted me to have a normal childhood. I had missed out on so much when I was younger that she just wanted me to enjoy being a normal kid.

★

In sixth grade, our school held a "team building day" which consisted of various teams competing in relay races, obstacle courses, and other activities that required participant cooperation. One of the events was a timed climb. The wall was about six or seven feet high–a foot or two higher than the tallest kid–with a wide ledge at the top. The challenge was to get all of your team over the wall as quickly as possible.

"No problem! Piece of cake!" the boys bragged, as they strutted around like hen-house roosters.

One by one, the biggest boys lifted and pushed the other kids up to the ledge until everyone was over the wall, or at least sitting on the ledge. Finally it was down to the last two boys. They hadn't really thought how best to get over themselves. One of the boys was able to push the other one up and over, but now he was stuck with no way to get himself over the wall.

"What are we going to do?" everyone worried. The clock was ticking, and the last boy was stuck at the bottom, jumping, trying to catch the hand of one of his cohorts.

"Tatyana can do it! Let Tatyana help! She can pull him up!" My girlfriends were aware of my other life with the Bennett Blazers. They knew I had become rather strong, but the boys never paid us any attention and weren't listening.

"We can do it! Where's Tatyana?" The girls were already motioning me back up onto the ledge. The boys realized we

Getting everyone over the wall.

were running out of time and had no other options.

"Hurry, Tatyana!"

I scrambled over to the edge. Holding onto me securely, my girlfriends lowered me down until I could reach the boy on the ground. I grabbed onto his forearms, slowly lifting him higher and higher until he was able to grab onto the top of the wall. There was a cheer from below. We had all made it over and won the competition!

On the way home from the event, Mom stopped so my friends and I could get ice cream sundaes. She pulled our van into a handicap parking spot to let us out.

"Oh, Ms. McFadden, you'll get a ticket for parking here!" one of my friends said worriedly.

"It's okay, we have a handicap sticker for Tatyana," she replied without giving much thought to it.

My friends looked at her and laughed. "Tatyana, handicapped? Hardly!"

Putting on the full court press.

CHAPTER 11

Athens

When eighth grade ended, I was a little uneasy about starting high school in the fall. It was a bigger school. I would have to make new friends and get used to new teachers. I tried to keep busy and distract myself from the feeling of butterflies in my stomach. Luckily, keeping busy was fairly easy to do. Racing had become more than a weekend activity. I had been competing in state and regional events with the Bennett Blazers and had already set U.S. records for my age group, in shot put, javelin, discus, and wheelchair racing.

I had dreamt that one day, maybe I could compete in the Olympics. I had heard about the Paralympics, which is

Out sightseeing at the Acropolis in Athens.

part of the Olympics and specifically created for people with disabilities. So it was a funny thing when after practice one day, Mr. Hughes, one of the field coaches, came over and asked me about my plans for the summer.

"Have you ever thought about racing in the Paralympics?"

"Yes, someday, I hope so!" I replied.

"No, I mean the Athens Paralympics, this coming September."

I was speechless. Was I ready to race in a worldwide competition that millions of people watch? I had just turned fifteen! I wasn't even in high school yet!

"I think you've got a good chance of qualifying for the U.S. team," he said. He explained that if I wanted to be considered I would have to send in the application form in two days. "If you get accepted, you'll get invited to race in the trials out in California to see if you qualify for the games. The trials are only a few weeks away!" he said in a tone of urgency.

"It shouldn't be difficult to get all the proper paperwork ready," he added. "Let me get you the forms, and you go talk to your mom."

It was Saturday, and the deadline was only two days away! It was already June, and the games were a little over two months away! Was it even possible? I ran off to find Mom.

Mom was a little skeptical, but, as usual, she wanted to support me in whatever I set my mind to. Had I said I was

What are the Paralympics?

The Paralympic Games are a major international multi-sport event for athletes with physical disabilities, including muscular dystrophy, spina bifida, and vision impairment.

The Games have grown from a small gathering of British World War II veterans in 1948 to one of the largest international sporting events today.

Both the Winter and Summer Paralympic Games are organized in parallel with the Olympic Games. Starting with the 1988 Summer Games in Seoul, South Korea, they have been held almost immediately after the respective Olympic Games.

starting a rock band, I am sure she would have bought me a set of drums. It was more of her you-can-do-anything way of thinking!

"What do we have to do?" she asked.

I explained to her about the application and Monday's deadline. The application needed to get the signature of a track official who could validate my fastest race times. We spent the rest of the weekend completing the forms. It was too late to send the letter by mail, so Mom faxed it to the Olympic headquarters in Colorado Springs on Monday morning. Now all I could do was to wait and cross my fingers!

Two weeks later a letter arrived from the Olympic Committee. My heart pounded as I opened the letter nervously and read:

"*Dear Tatyana, This letter is to inform you that you have qualified to attend the trials for the U.S. Paralympics Team to possibly compete in the 2004 Paralympic Games in Athens, Greece.*"

I couldn't believe what I was reading! My mind was spinning!

"Tatyana, this says the trials are in two weeks!" Mom said as she skimmed over the letter.

"There's so much to do... I don't know." She added hesitantly, "And it's in California!"

By the time I was aware of what she was saying, Mom was already on her computer looking for airfares to the West Coast.

✳

Two weeks later Mom and I were at the racetrack at the Spartan Stadium in San Jose, California. The other racers were gathering, and the time trials were beginning.

"It's great you were able to come out and learn about the Paralympics," one of the older athletes said with a smile.

I didn't think she meant to sound as dismissive or condescending as she did. But after a few more "greetings" like this from the other athletes, I was losing my confidence. After all, I was only fifteen. Most of the athletes were in their twenties and thirties and had been working with professional coaches for years. Even my own mother viewed my going to the trials as "good experience" more than actually a chance to qualify for the Games in Athens.

"Mom, what am I going to do?" My voice was shaking. I usually didn't get this nervous before competitions.

"Just do the best you can!" she said reassuringly.

I told myself that if I didn't race well, we'd go home, and in four years I could try out again. At least I wouldn't be the "newbie" on the track then.

Based on my track times from the track meets back home I had qualified to race in the trials for the 100-, 200-, 400-, and 800-meter sprints. The 100- and 200-meters were short sprints and were all about upper-body strength. They were my best chance to qualify. I knew I was fast out of the starting gates. I hoped I was fast enough to keep up with the other racers. The 400- and 800-meter races would be harder. It takes a lot of endurance to keep up the speed for those longer distances.

"Mom!" I looked at my mother with more than a little fear and apprehension.

"Sweetie, just run fast!"

"Runners, ready on the course!" the announcer said.

I headed onto the track and started to relax. Here on the track I was in my element.

The other racers weren't staring at me anymore. Everyone focused on the race.

"*Runners on your mark!*"

"CRACK!" went the starting gun. I sprang out of the gate, pushing on the wheels as fast as I could as we raced down the straightaway.

"*Ya sama! Ya sama!*" I repeated again and again.

I was aware of the other racers on either side of me. I was keeping up, but it was going to be close. I couldn't tell if anyone was in the lead. Everything was moving so fast.

"*I can do it! I can do it!*"

Almost to the finish line, I put on an extra burst of speed and crossed ahead of the others.

The other racers gasped for air, exhausted and sinking back into their chairs. I was tired too, but exhilarated from my first race. On the scoreboard above the track the names of the winners came up: *First place—Tatyana McFadden*.

Everyone looked at me with a mix of shock and surprise. I had won! *I was going to Athens!*

✶

The most amazing thing I remember about the Athens Games was the number of athletes participating. Four thousand competitors from all over the world, all with disabilities! It was thrilling to see so many people, like me, running, jumping, swimming, throwing.

At the opening ceremony I paraded into the stadium

Opening Ceremony at the Athens Paralympics.

with the U.S. team and teams from 135 other countries. There were thousands of people above us in the stadium, cheering and flashing cameras. I was ecstatic. It was wonderful to be representing my adopted country, America.

The president of the International Paralympic Committee began to speak.

"*You set standards and give expression for many people...around the world....*" he declared.

The words echoed over the loudspeakers and filled my head. I had never thought much about setting standards for anyone else. I could barely clean my room much less set standards for myself! I competed in sports events because I loved doing it. But in that moment, surrounded by so many incredible athletes, being cheered by the thousands

Family and friends cheering me on!

of fans, I felt something grow inside me. As corny as it might sound, in that moment I experienced a new desire to make a difference. I realized that through my actions I could inspire and help others. I wasn't quite sure exactly how I might do it, but something special had happened in the opening ceremonies.

✶

I had qualified to race in the 100-, 200-, 400-, and 800-meter races. My first race was the 100-meter, which was my strongest event. I knew if there was any hope of me winning a medal, it was in this race. I was all nerves waiting for it to start.

When my family and friends heard I was competing in the Paralympics, they all decided to come to Athens.

"We know you can do it! Remember, Tatyana, we'll all be there cheering you on!" my Grandma Jo said enthusiastically.

"How will I know where you are, Grandma?" I asked.

"Don't worry, we'll get to the stadium early and get good seats. We'll all be wearing white t-shirts. Look for the banner!" They had made t-shirts that read "Go Tatyana Go!" for everyone and a big banner with my name on it.

Eleven women including myself had qualified to compete in the 100-meter race, so two preliminary races, or heats, would determine the top six racers to race in the finals. I was in the first heat with six of the competitors. The other racers all looked so much older than me! I tried to focus on my breathing as I settled into position in my racing chair.

"...on your mark!"

"CRACK!" went the starting gun.

We were off! I bounded off the starting line. I quickly took the lead and crossed the finish line in 16.71 seconds! I won the first heat! I was a clear half second ahead of the next racer.

As I caught my breath I watched the remaining five racers line up for the second heat. Chantal Petitclerc, one of Canada's top wheelchair racers won the heat in 16.45

seconds. I had earned a place in the finals, but I knew that to win I needed to at least beat her time.

The next day, I was feeling confident but nervous. On the track getting into position, I glanced at Chantal.

"*Runners, on your mark!*"

"CRACK!"

Chantal pulled out quickly, with me following closely behind her. I knew I could do it. Just a fraction of a second difference...down to the finish, I could see it.

"*Now push!* YA SAMA!"

I thrust my arms on the wheels harder and faster, but at the same moment Chantal gave it her last thrust. I was just beside her. It would be close...

Heading around the last turn.

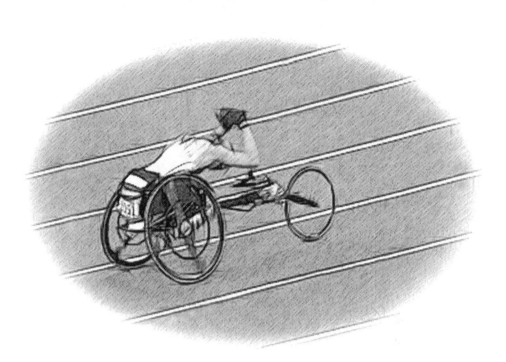

Second place! I did it!

"In first place, Chantal Petitclerc, in second place, Tatyana McFadden...."

Second place! I had won second place! Chantal had won the gold, but I had won a silver medal in the Paralympics! I was so excited! Not bad for a fifteen-year-old!

✶

I was the youngest member of the U.S. Paralympic Track and Field Team that year, and I came home with the silver medal for the 100-meter run and a bronze medal for the 200-meter race.

High school had already started by the time I returned home from the Athens. When I arrived for my

Me and Chantal in a celebratory hug.

first day of high school, the marquee in front of the school read: "Congratulations, Tatyana McFadden!" A week later, a letter addressed to me arrived from the White House! The president of the United States had written to congratulate me! Then the local newspaper called to request an interview. And to top it all off I was invited to ride in my high school homecoming parade. What a great way to start the school year!

CHAPTER 12

Kids Like You!

I had thought my freshman year was going to be much harder to adjust to, but I had obtained a bit of celebrity status. I made lots of new friends and what might have been viewed as my disability was seen as part of my unique abilities by the other students.

I was still competing in basketball and track with the Bennett Blazers and in the spring of my freshman year, I joined my high school's track team. I remembered the school principal encouraging everyone at freshman orientation to get involved in sports. All my friends were joining teams, and I hadn't thought it would be much of a problem

Practicing on my own.

to join the track team.

Usually anyone who wants to can join a high school track team. Unlike football or baseball teams which have a limited number of positions, there is always room for another pole vaulter, high jumper, or sprinter. I couldn't pole vault and I couldn't high jump, but put me on the racetrack and well...I did have two Paralympic medals.

"Sorry," the athletic director told me, "but you can't race with the team. There are clubs for kids like you." He didn't say it in a particularly mean way. He just stated what he knew to be a fact. He shrugged his shoulders and gave me a "there's nothing I can do" look as he walked away.

When I decide I want to do something—no matter how difficult—I figure out a way to do it. All of my friends were racing, and I wanted to race with them!

Maybe I wasn't *officially* part of the team, but the track was a public place. As long as I didn't get in the way of the team and the coach, I decided there was no harm in practicing alongside them.

Each day after school, I showed up at the racetrack. I raced alone. The track coach didn't seem to mind. After a while he occasionally used me to pace the other runners as they were practicing.

"Just keep up with Tatyana!" he instructed them.

Eventually the coach gave me a uniform to wear. One afternoon he announced that our team had been invited to race in a track meet at a nearby school. It was the first meet of the season, and there would be at least four or five other schools competing.

"Everyone must be at the school parking lot on Saturday morning at 6:30. The bus leaves at 6:45 sharp!" he announced.

"The coach had said everyone," I thought to myself. I had put so much time into practicing. He must have seen what a good athlete I was and expected me to race too. Great!

Bright and early Saturday morning, my mom took me to the school parking lot. All the kids were boarding the bus. Mom helped me load my wheelchair, and I hopped aboard with my friends for the trip to my first high school track meet!

High school track meets are often not very exciting events (especially compared to the Paralympics!). This was the first meet of the year, and it was an invitational meet, which means it didn't count toward scoring team points for the regional trophy. Events happen simultaneously, pole vaulting in one corner of the field, shot putting and javelin in another, while the runners run around the track competing in one race after another.

There weren't many people in the bleachers. It was mostly families of the hosting team, watching intently to see how a son or daughter was doing. Most were hanging out in their seats, chatting with neighbors and enjoying the morning.

I stretched and raced a few practice loops around the

track. I didn't know when I was racing, but I figured at some point someone would let me know.

The race official shouted out the names of each competitor, occasionally glancing over at me with a quizzical look on his face. I was feeling anxious and listened intently for my name.

"Excuse me," I politely asked. "When do I race?"

The man looked at me and then down at his clipboard, turning over the pages several times.

"I see nothing about a wheelchair race listed here, miss. Are you sure you were supposed to race today?"

"Yes, I'm here, aren't I? My name is Tatyana McFadden. Maybe there's a mistake?" I asked with as much confidence as I could muster.

"Hmm. I don't see your name here anywhere..." His voice trailed off.

"Must be an oversight!" he said cheerfully, and added my name to the roster. I learned later that he also officiated in New Jersey where wheelchair racers often race along with the other runners, so this was no big deal to him.

"Let's see, how about the women's 400-meter race, just once around the track? It's coming up next. Make sure you stay in the outside lane!" he said. I nodded happily.

"Women's 400-meter!" came the announcement over the loudspeaker.

I was excited. I took off my warm-up jacket and tossed it on the bench.

"Holy smokes! Look at those guns!" I heard one man say, jabbing his elbow into the man next to him and pointing at my muscular arms. I had strong arms for a girl and it showed, especially now that they were pumped up from stretching and doing a few practice runs.

I set up in the outside lane and pushed down onto the wheels of my chair, ready to spring out of the starting gate. There was some commotion going on in the bleachers. Everyone was looking at me!

"Runners on your mark!"

"CRACK!" went the starting gun.

We were off! I was lagging behind the others at the start. Unlike running on your feet, racing in a chair takes more effort at the start to get the wheels moving. For the first 100 meters I was behind most of the other runners, but I kept pushing. Bit by bit, I caught up. By the end of the first quarter I was trailing just a little. Halfway around the track I passed the slowest runners.

"Go, girl! Go! You can do it!" the crowd yelled. They had put down their newspapers and were following the race. They were cheering me along!

I was neck-and-neck with the fastest runners as we went into the final quarter of the race. It would be close!

"All right! You go, girl! Go! You got it!" I heard coming from the bleachers.

It was down around the last turn and into the final stretch of the race. The crowd was on its feet screaming and clapping!

Only seconds to the finish line, I made one last strong rocket-like blast.

"Tatyana McFadden, first place, wheelchair division, 400-meter race!"

I had won! The crowd cheered and clapped, and my friends ran over to congratulate me.

"Great race, great race!"

After the race I called my Grandpa.

"Hi, Tatyana, how'd the race go?"

"Great, Grandpa! It's the best day in my whole life!" I was so happy.

"Why's that?" he asked.

"Because I got to ride the bus with my friends!"

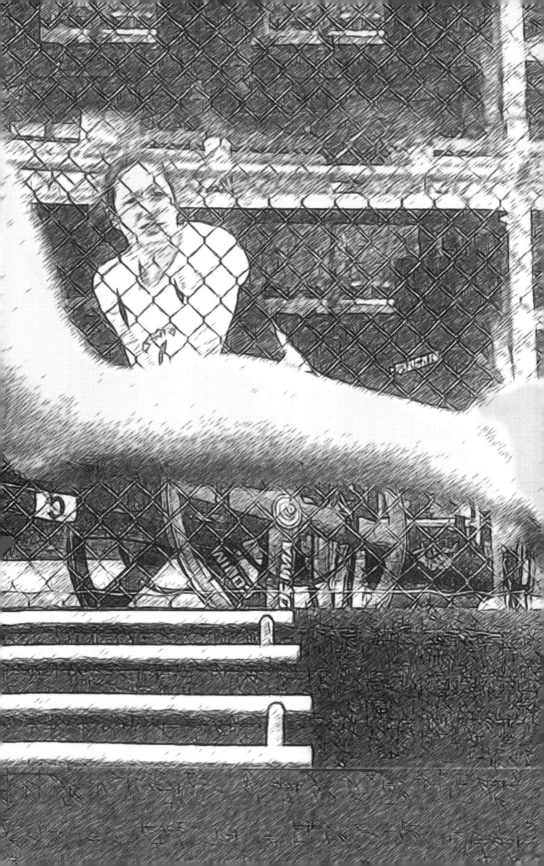

CHAPTER 13

She's Different, Your Honor!

Mom, they won't let me work out with the team anymore!"

When the coach said everyone should go to the meet, I thought he meant me too, but it turned out I was wrong.

"What's wrong with me?" I cried. "Doesn't everyone mean *everyone*?"

It had been three days since the track meet, and I'd been feeling great about the race and earning a place on the team. Back at school on Monday morning, the athletic director called me into his office. He had heard what had happened at the track meet.

"I'm sorry, Tatyana, but you can't race with the team,"

waiting for my chance to race.

he said. "The track team is for runners. You know, there are other groups you can join." I couldn't tell if he was trying to be helpful or was being dismissive.

I was shaken up when I left his office and spent the rest of the day on the verge of tears. I loved racing. I couldn't figure out why he wouldn't want me on our high school's track team. I couldn't even practice with them.

"Maybe I can talk to him," my mom said, trying to comfort me. I don't think Mom had ever seen me this upset. "I'll go speak to him tomorrow," she promised. "I'm sure we can work something out."

✶

The next afternoon I went with my mom to see the athletic director.

"Here, please sit down." He pulled out a chair for her and then slipped back around his desk and sat down. Behind him was a shelf of team trophies and medals along with photos of his favorite athletes.

"Sorry to be a bother to you," Mom said, "but Tatyana wants to be on the team, and she says you won't allow it."

"I'm sorry, Ms. McFadden. It isn't me, it's just school policy," he said.

My mom tried to reason with him, but as he had told me the day before, it wasn't his decision to make.

"Let me go speak to the principal," Mom told me as we drove home. Now she was upset, and I was totally crushed.

Mom had taught me that there were no doors closed to me. And this seemed so unfair. Track is not like football or basketball where you have to try out to be on the team. With track, anyone who shows up can participate. All I wanted was to have what any other student in my school had—the opportunity to race.

Later in the week we went to see the school principal and got a similar response.

"I'm very sorry, Ms. McFadden," she said, "but it's school district policy. Tatyana can't be on the track team. I know it doesn't make sense but, perhaps..." she paused, "you could try taking it up with the county school board."

So mom went to the school board, but again was met with resistance.

"It's against the law not to let my daughter be on the high school track team," my mother explained to them. "It's discrimination."

✶

Mom, it's not right," I said, frustrated. "Is there anything we can do?"

"If you truly want this," she told me, "we can file a grievance with the courts, and a judge will decide if you can be on the team or not. It won't be easy. It's a lot of work, and we might ruffle a few feathers."

I hesitated, thinking about what she was saying. I had no idea what the outcome might be. On the one hand,

I wanted to race with my friends at school, but I also had the Bennett Blazers and had won two Paralympic medals already. My racing life was hardly over. And whatever happened at my school wasn't going to stop me.

But then I thought about other kids with disabilities. I had been fortunate to be involved in sports from an early age, and I knew how much it had improved my life. But what about other kids who didn't have the support and encouragement I had? I realized this wasn't only about me. It was my chance to help others in the same situation.

"Let's do it!" I said anxiously.

Mom went to Maryland Disability Law Center, which helps defend the civil rights of people with disabilities, and the lawsuit *Tatyana McFadden vs. Howard County School District* was filed. Most lawsuits sue for damages, which means the person with the complaint asks for money from the person they are suing. I didn't want money. I wanted the right to race alongside my high school track team.

When word got around that I was suing the school, most students were supportive. But the teachers and coaches had mixed reactions. Some didn't understand what I was doing or why. Others thought that if I won the lawsuit, it would end up costing the school district more money than it could afford to accommodate students with disabilities into their sports programs.

Once the suit was filed, a ruling was made that allowed me to keep racing in school track meets until the case could be heard in court. But rather than let me compete with the other runners, someone at my school decided that if I had to race, then I would race alone. At the next race, as I went around the track, only a few people cheered me on. It was hardly exciting to watch.

"Boo!" someone shouted from the bleachers as I came around the last turn to the finish line.

I felt so embarrassed, but tried not to let it bother me. Even so, the last few feet of that race were some of the most difficult few feet I've ever raced!

✳

This court is called to order! Tatyana McFadden vs. Howard County School District," the clerk announced across the courtroom.

The judge entered the courtroom, and everyone rose. I pushed myself up in my wheelchair, sitting up as straight as I possibly could. As he sat down, the judge glanced over at me and then at the two lawyers who were representing the school. I am sure it looked strange to him—a fifteen year-old-girl in a wheelchair defending herself against two men in suits. The hearing started with testimony from several experts on sports and disabilities who spoke on my behalf about the importance of including kids with disabilities in school sports programs. We showed a video of me warming up with my teammates before a meet, then a video of me racing around the track alone once the meet started.

After our presentation the judge turned to the two lawyers for the school. As best as I can remember, the conversation went something like this—

"Can you tell me what's going on?" he asked.

"We don't know, your honor. We let Miss McFadden race."

"You didn't let her race. You let her run around the course by herself, did you not?" he retorted.

"That's because she's different, Your Honor."

"So you are telling me you think people who are different should be separated from each other?"

"Yes, Your Honor!" both attorneys quickly shot back without hesitation.

The judge sat silent for a moment and shook his head in dismay. They had just admitted I was being singled out and treated differently, which is the definition of discrimination! The judge's questioning went on for almost five hours. It took several weeks for his ruling to be announced—in my favor on the grounds of discrimination. We had won! The story made the newspapers nationwide.

But the victory was short lived. Almost immediately after, the Maryland Public Secondary Schools Athletic Association declared that wheelchair racing would be permitted in school sports throughout Maryland, but only as an "exhibition sport" and would not be considered part of the competition. This still felt like discrimination to me. Every disabled student should be allowed to compete equally in school athletics.

"Nobody should have to go through what I just experienced!" I said with exasperation over dinner one night.

"Well..." my mom was busy thinking again. "If you're willing to do the work it will take, we can try and get a state law passed that would make it harder to exclude people with disabilities."

Over the next six months, with the help of local sports groups, civil rights organizations, and lawyers who had been encouraged by my court case, we drafted a bill that would allow students with disabilities to participate in their school athletic programs. In order for the bill to become law, it would need to be voted on and approved by the Maryland

In the courtroom.

state legislature. This meant we had to build support among individual state representatives and senators. It would take many months of hard work before the bill was presented to the state legislature for a vote. I met with as many people in the state government as I could.

"How would you feel if your daughter or son was in a wheelchair and they couldn't play with their friends?" I asked courteously, smiling, from my wheelchair. I have to admit, I was hard to resist!

After two years in the making, the Fitness and Athletics Equity for Students with Disabilities Act was passed in the spring of 2008. The law ensured that Maryland school sports programs not only included kids with disabilities, but that they be treated equally to other students. This guaranteed that no one could be sidelined and given a balloon to hold in gym class like I was years before. Often called "Tatyana's Law," the act has inspired similar changes in state laws across the country.

It had been a tense time at school for me as well as the students and teachers who were opposed to the lawsuit. But eventually everyone came around when they saw that including kids with disabilities in regular sports activities was much easier than they had imagined.

Sometimes, people just need to be challenged on what they think is possible. All it takes is the willingness to try something new and a little imagination to figure out how to make it happen.

CHAPTER 14

For the Win

I was only a sophomore in high school, but I was now considered an "elite athlete"—a term that means I was a professional athlete who had competed in national and international competitions. I was racing with both my high school track team and the Bennett Blazers and competing around the world. It was a lot to juggle!

I was getting more serious about my training and crafting my racing skills. Most elite athletes have personal coaches whose full-time job is training their athlete. I didn't have a personal coach, but I had my family for emotional support and my coaches from the Bennett Blazers and my high school track team to help me improve my racing skills. Everyone gave me advice, which I tried to absorb so I could

Getting serious on the track.

become a better athlete.

"To be a good racer you need to race fast, but to be a great racer you need to race smart," my coach advised me. "Watch the other racers. Learn their strengths and weaknesses as well as your own."

I listened and learned.

"You need to better understand each race," another coach advised. "How you race the 100-meter race is going to be very different from how you race the 800 or 1500."

One of the interesting things I discovered was that I could use wind resistance to help me win. When you are going fast in a racing chair, the chair creates a *slipstream*—a wave of air that pushes out to both sides of the racing chair. It's like the wake of a speedboat.

When racers create a slipstream, they also create a *draft* directly behind the race chair. If you've ever walked into a windstorm and then ducked behind someone, you can understand how wind can play a big role in how fast you can move. The person in front blocks the wind and makes it easier for you to walk.

Race right behind someone, protected in their draft, and it takes less effort to keep up with them. Race slightly to the side of another race chair, and you can surf the slipstream like a wave.

When I first started racing I didn't pay much attention to slipstream and draft. Once I got on the track, my goal was to get out and race as fast as I could. This wasn't a

The science behind racing

The DRAFT is the area right behind a racing chair where there is less wind resistance. Riding in the draft is like walking behind someone in a windstorm.

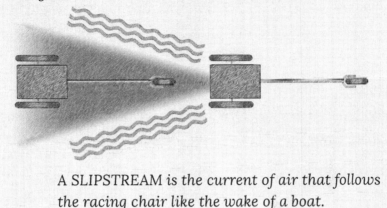

A SLIPSTREAM is the current of air that follows the racing chair like the wake of a boat.

bad strategy. I was winning medals, but I was fairly new to professional racing and still had a lot to learn. It was in the 2006 IPC World Championships in the Netherlands when I decided to apply some of what I had learned about wind resistance, slipstreams, and draft.

"Stay behind in the first half of the race and ride in the draft," I overheard someone say, sharing her strategy for winning. "Save your energy for the last push, and you can totally win it!"

It made sense. I knew how to go into overdrive right before the finish line, but if I could conserve my energy for the big push at the end it might shave off the few seconds that would mean a win.

"Runners on your mark!"

The crowd went silent as we locked ourselves in position on the track. The seconds clicked down.

"CRACK!" the starting gun went off, and I exploded off the starting line. The crowd erupted in cheers and shouts as we raced into the straightaway. Everyone scrambled to get into the inside lanes. I pulled behind one of the other racers, tucked my front wheel just beneath her racing chair, and settled into her draft. Around me the other racers moved and jockeyed for position, trying to take advantage of the draft and the slipstreams of the racers in front.

The wheels of my chair were so close to the other racers' wheels. One slight move too close could send my chair tumbling over and cause a major pile-up!

Through the first, second, and third laps, I kept close behind the racing chair in front of me. Then we headed into the final lap.

"Time to move out ahead!" I thought.

I dropped back a little and started to break out from the group. To the right and left of me the other racers weren't budging. I was boxed in! Stuck! I couldn't move out! I was even wedged in from behind!

I started panicking. There wasn't enough time or distance to slow down to let the others pass and then pull out and race around them. We went around the last turn, and everyone suddenly spread out for the sprint to the finish line. Finally, I was free of the congestion! Ahead of me, I could see at least four other racers.

"*Faster, faster!*" I screamed to myself, gaining some ground on the other racers. But I was too late.

I don't even remember what position I came in, only that it wasn't first, it wasn't second, and it wasn't even third place.

I could have, I should have won it! I hadn't even raced at my top speed. I had been totally cut off by the other racers. I was angry and frustrated. I wanted to cry.

While the other racers all gathered around high-fiving and congratulating one another, I felt like the wind had been knocked out of me—not from the exertion of the race but because I had lost. I escaped to the warm-up track behind the stadium where I knew I could be alone and cry.

"You okay?" a voice called out.

It was Chantal Petitclerc, the Canadian racer who had beaten me in Athens and won the gold medal. I didn't know her well, but she was one of the top racers and one of my biggest competitors.

"You okay?" she asked again as she came up beside me and gave me a reassuring pat on the back.

"I'll be fine." My wet and reddened eyes said otherwise, but I tried to smile.

"It was a good race. You tried your best. You can't let one loss get you so upset." She was trying to be consoling.

"But they boxed me in..." I said in a defeated voice.

She quickly figured out that I wasn't upset about

losing. I was upset about the fact that the other athletes had cut me off.

"Look, you need to understand something. No one did anything to make you lose," she explained. "When the starting gun goes off, it's everyone for herself. Nothing personal about it! Remember—there is only one first place. Your problem is you assumed they would open up for you so you could win. They all wanted to win too. There was no conspiracy against you. You got boxed in—that's all," she said sympathetically.

I hadn't thought about it in that way. I looked up at her. Her face was calm and smiling, her voice was reassuring. Here she was—one of the top racers in the world and one of my competitors—trying to cheer me up and give me some wise advice! My nerves were still frayed, and I was exhausted from feeling sorry for myself, but I knew she was right. I lost, but it wasn't anything someone else had done to me. This was a competition.

"Yeah, I guess I screwed up." I smiled and then let out a tiny laugh. My ego was bruised, and I was still mad, but now it was anger at myself for being outmaneuvered. Lesson learned!

✶

Over the next few years I paid more attention to the other competitors and how they raced and also got to know their personalities better. Each had a unique pattern of behavior on the racetrack. Working with my coach, I tried to become a smarter racer, which meant better understanding when I should pull back and when I should race ahead. Over time, I started to build my own strategy for success. Slowly but surely, I picked up more and more wins.

By the London Paralympics in 2012—six years after my loss in the Netherlands—I had improved my strength and my speed, but my usual strategy was still to get out in front of the pack, "pulling" some racers in my draft and letting others ride my slipstream. The upside of this was that I never had to worry about being boxed in. The downside was that I could exhaust myself faster than the other racers and let someone else slip ahead of me on the final stretch to win the race.

In London, I was racing again in the 1500-meter event. I had studied the times of the other racers and knew it would be a close race. Working with my coach, I decided to try something new.

Once again we were all in position on the starting line. I was in the second lane.

"CRACK!" went the gun and we were off! We pulled into the first straightaway, everyone moving toward the inside lanes. I held back slightly. The other racers slowed, waiting for me to pull into the lead as usual. They were ready to ride in my draft. But I stayed toward the back, moving to the outside, which forced the others to move out front and to the inside of the track.

Hanging with my teammates.

First, second, and third lap I kept toward the back and outside of the other racers. We moved into the last lap, and everyone began to push it out hard. Being in the outside lane, I could see a direct line to the front without having to worry too much about maneuvering around the other racers. I needed to surge out now and put on the burn! Three hundred meters to the finish line, and I passed at least half of the other racers. Two hundred meters to go, and I was just coming up on the front-runner.

"Ya sama! Ya sama!" I chanted over and over to myself. My hands pushed harder and faster on the rims of my racing chair. I shortened my stroke as I hit the final stretch to quicken my pace. My hands shot off the push rims and down, again and again. I could see the finish line ahead as I passed the front runner! *I did it!*

It was one of three gold medals I won that year in the London Paralympics. I had come a long way from that losing race in the Netherlands. I now better understood how to win—it was both a physical and a mental race. And I better understood my own mind and body, and those of my competitors.

Losing taught me a valuable lesson. It's easy to blame others, or a faulty wheel, or the weather, or even not getting a good sleep the night before. I realized that there will always be excuses and disappointments, but I can't go off in a corner and wallow in self-pity. When I don't do as well as I hoped in a race, I remember it's only a race. In the bigger picture of my life, I am always winning.

CHAPTER 15

Make a Difference

I graduated from high school in 2008, with many successes under my wheels. I was offered a sports scholarship to the University of Illinois at Urbana-Champaign. I'd applied to several schools, but the Urbana-Champaign campus was my first choice because they had one of the top facilities in the country for athletes with disabilities.

I was very familiar with the school as I had spent several of my high school summers at their sports camp, training with their head track coach, Adam Bleakney. Adam is an incredible athlete whom I had first competed against in Athens. He had just been named U.S. Paralympic Coach of

Visiting an orphanage in Russia.

the Year in 2007, and I knew he could push my skills to the next level.

I was also excited about the Urbana-Champaign campus because they have a great child development and family studies program. I had an incredible—and sometimes challenging—childhood, and I was fortunate to have been supported by family and friends who helped make me who I am today. I now wanted to help other children and their families, who might face challenges like mine in their own lives.

Since the scholarship was for basketball and track, during the fall basketball season I practiced basketball each morning and in the afternoon wheelchair racing. It was a grueling schedule to handle on top of my college classes. By spring, after basketball season was over, I focused all my efforts on track. It was at Adam's suggestion that I start training to race in marathons.

"Just think of it as racing fifty 800-meter sprints, one after another! Only pace yourself a bit. You'll figure it out," he said.

I hadn't really thought much about racing marathons. I had always been best at sprinting, my favorite being the 800-meter race. Fifty 800-meter sprints. I was ready for the challenge!

Each morning I was up and on the racetrack by about 6:30 a.m. doing my sprints, one after another to build up my strength. Then I switched over to distance racing to build my stamina. By the following year, Adam was referring to me as "The Beast." I didn't love the name, but I did seem to have an unusual reserve power that I could turn on in the crucial moments of a race to push out ahead of my competition.

That fall, in October 2009, I raced in my first marathon in Chicago and won, beating out the second place winner by just two-tenths of a second!

I always assumed my strength was in my short-distance racing skills but after that first marathon win, I went on to win in other marathons across the country and Europe, including the Grand Slam (Chicago, Boston, London, and New York City) in 2013, 2014, and 2015. Within a few years I was recognized as one of the top marathon racers in the country.

✷

You're my daughter's hero," I read in an email a few weeks before the 2013 Chicago marathon. "Her name is Addison and she is going to turn five in a few weeks. We live in Chicago. If it's possible, she'd really like to meet you!"

This message was from one of a half-dozen fan emails I received each week. I couldn't imagine I had such an enthusiastic four-year-old fan, but something in the email caught my interest so I responded.

"My schedule is pretty busy," I emailed, "but I could meet for a few minutes right after the press conference on the day before the marathon."

I didn't know what to expect. The press conference was being held in the ballroom of the hotel where I was staying. I was just finishing up an interview, and most of the press had moved on to talk to some of the other athletes.

"It's Tatyana McFadden!" a tiny voice screamed out. "It's Tatyana! My hero!"

From across the room a little blonde-haired girl wearing bright turquoise glasses was speeding toward me in her red wheelchair. Every head in the room turned to look at the child who was screaming my name.

"Tatyana! Tatyana!" She wheeled right up to me and without any hesitation gave me a big hug.

A few of the reporters came over to us. One of them put Addison in front of the video camera and began interviewing her.

"I'm Addison Zellner and I'm four years old and I'm going to be five and Tatyana McFadden is my best friend. Someday I want to grow up and be just like her and race!"

She was so determined and direct! I asked her if she wanted to race me across the hotel lobby.

"Oh, yes! Please, can we?" she cried eagerly.

I had noticed a long, empty hallway behind the lobby. It was wide enough so that we probably wouldn't run down any hotel guests who might walk through. Several of the hotel staff who had been watching us put a linen napkin at the far end of the hall to mark a finish line. They stood guard in the corridor to make sure no one walked across our track. Then Addison and I lined up on the starting line.

"*On your mark...get set, go!*"

Addison raced out ahead of me, and I followed closely behind her, catching up to her as she crossed the napkin finish line.

"Yes, I won! I won!" She shouted triumphantly and flashed me a look of pride and the biggest grin. She had beaten Tatyana McFadden!

One of the marathon race directors came over to us.

"Addison, would you like to have tickets to be at the finish line tomorrow?" he asked. These tickets were very hard to get, but Addison's enthusiasm was so infectious. I took a back seat as Addison continued to engage the crowd, answering questions with the seriousness of a pro athlete. I might be her role model, but at that moment she was the one who inspired me.

"Addison, I'm going to dedicate this marathon to you!" I told her as we said goodbye.

★

The day of the Chicago marathon was freezing. Halfway through the race I was in the lead. I crossed the finish line in one hour and forty-four minutes to win the race—only twenty-two seconds ahead of the second-place winner.

Addison was waiting for me, bundled up in a thick pink-and-white parka and a big woolly hat. Her turquoise glasses poked out of the bundle.

"Tatyana! Tatyana! You won! You won!" she cried in excitement, greeting me with a big hug.

I remember how I felt at her age, and how excited I was seeing my first race on my first day in America, getting "high-fived" by the passing runners. And also how lucky I had been to have had so many people throughout my life to inspire and encourage me. I took my first-place medal from around my neck and placed it over Addison's head.

"Here, Addison, this is for you."

"Oh, Tatyana. Thank you, thank you!"

I am sure everyone watching us was a little taken aback at how casually I gave away the medal I had only just received to a little girl I had only just met. It wasn't that the medal didn't mean anything to me. It was actually because it meant so much to me that I gave it to Addison. I hoped it might inspire her to do great things in her own life.

Before that moment I had been aware I had fans and that some people followed me in the news as if I were a celebrity. But I hadn't fully realized that I was making a difference by serving as a role model for kids like Addison.

✶

Me and Addison at the Chicago Marathon.

Mom once read a story to me. I have since heard it many times, and it's still so special to me. It goes something like this:

One morning a young boy was walking along a beach when he came across thousands of starfish that had washed ashore. He sees an old man walking slowly along the beach, picking up one starfish after another and tossing each one back into the sea.

"Why are you throwing the starfish back into the ocean?" the boy asks.

"Because the sun is coming up and the tide is going out and if I don't throw them back into the ocean they will die."

"But, there are miles and miles of beach and there are thousands of starfish all along it! You can't possibly save them all, you can't even save one tenth of them. In fact, even if you work all day, it won't make any difference at all."

The old man listened politely and then bent down, picked up another starfish, and gently threw it into the sea.

"It made a difference to that one."

✴

I was that little starfish on the beach! Throughout my life it has been the efforts and intentions, both grand and small, of the people around me who have made my hopes and dreams possible. Surrounded by such love and support, I have found the power to be anything I want to be.

Now, I hope I can help others realize their own power to be anything that they want to be. *YA SAMA!*

My Family Album

There is so much about my life and family that I wanted to tell but just couldn't fit into this book. So I thought I would share a few more snapshots of my life and the incredible people who surround me. Enjoy!

Making
friends.

Mara, me, Elana, and
my sister Hannah.
Mara and Elana were
adopted from Russia
at the same time I was.

Ice skating
with friends

Girl Scout
Brownies.

Clowning
around!

Some of the people I have met on my journey.

Prince Harry presenting me with the trophy at the London Marathon.

Meeting Michael Phelps.

Justin Bieber photobombs my pic!

On the runway at ESPN's glitzy ESPY Awards.

2014 Paralympics in Sochi, Russia. My first time competing in a winter sport and revisiting my past. More about that in my next book!

Racing the one-kilometer cross-country skiing race.

Crossing the finish line, exhausted!

And the winners are: 1. Ukraine, 2. USA 3. Russia.

Celebration dinner after my win.

A congratulatory hug from one of my sponsors.

Natalya, who looked after me at the orphanage.

From the USA to Russia, my inspiration, my family!

Pasha helping me down
the stairs on my last
day in Russia.

Twenty years later at the
winter Paralympics in Sochi,
Russia, Pasha helps me
navigate some difficult stairs!

In training at the University of Illinois.

Taking on a dare to see if I could pull a car! I did!

Sporting my winning laurels.

Me and my coach Adam Bleakney.

Competing with my
sister Hannah at the
London Paralympics.

My sister Ruthi and
me exploring India.

Me with
Grandma Jo.

Sisters!

At the Great Wall of China
with friends and family.

My Bennett Blazers
teammates, now all competing
at the University of Illinois.

My family at
the Taj Mahal.

Afterword

In the course of creating this memoir, I have reached
out to many of my friends to add clarity and detail
to my own memories. In some instances I have simplified
events to better capture the spirit of a particular time
or place in my life.

Acknowledgements

Life is not a journey of one, but a journey of many. It is a journey filled with family, friends, caregivers, coaches, and teammates, all of whom enrich my life. I hope, in some small way, that this book pays tribute to them.

I am grateful to my birth mother, who gave me life; Natalya Vasalya, who watched over me in the orphanage; Gwena and Gerry Herman and the Bennett Blazers, who introduced me to the world of sports and encouraged me to try every sport imaginable; Lauren Young of Maryland Disability Law Center, who stood by me as I fought for equality on my high school track team; Adam Bleakney, my coach at the University of Illinois, who inspires, challenges, and helps me to be my best on the track and in life; my teammates and friends, who bring joy to my life in so many ways; my loyal and crazy fans, who cheer me on all over the world; my sponsors, who have helped make it possible for me to train and compete; my mothers, Deborah McFadden and Bridget O'Shaughnessey, who believe there are no limits to what I can achieve; my grandparents, aunts, uncles, cousins, extended family, and friends who continue to support and encourage me; and most importantly my incredible sisters, Hannah and Ruthi, who remind me every day that family is everything—I love you to the moon and back.

And my sincere appreciation to the people who helped put this book together: Tom Walker, who took the time to listen to my story and accurately capture it in the written word; my editors, Ann Carper and Laura Markowitz; and editorial assistant Scott Larimer.

- *Tatyana McFadden*

Resources

Sports are important to all kids but especially kids who face challenges in their lives. At the top of the list of organizations that helped me are the Girl Scouts and the Bennett Blazers. Both groups taught me not only about sports but also about friendship and community. Here are a few resources to help you get started in sports.

Bennett Blazers   www. bennettblazers.org
Girl Scouts   www.girlscouts.org
USA Paralympics   www.usparalympic.org
Adaptive Sports   www.adaptivesportsfoundation.org
Disabled Sports USA   www.disabledsportsusa.org

You can also find more resources at my website:
www.tatyanamcfadden.com

About InspiredEdge Editions

Established in 2015, InspiredEdge Editions
creates and publishes books and other content,
across both traditional and digital media,
to inspire and educate people of all ages through
tales of triumph in the face of adversity.

www.ieeditions.com`

Made in the USA
Middletown, DE
13 May 2016